CONTENTS

CW00420215

i

FOREWORD

In June 1994, amidst considerable publicity, The Scottish Office launched a media campaign on the topic of domestic violence. The main aims of the campaign were: to highlight the criminality of domestic violence and foster an atmosphere of public condemnation towards the perpetrators of such violence; to encourage perpetrators to think about the consequences and implications of their behaviour; and to provide information about support for those affected by domestic violence.

The campaign had three main components. At its core was a forty second **television commercial**, shown intensively over a 5 week period in June and July 1994 and repeated intermittently over the period October-December 1994. A ten second follow-up to the main commercial provided viewers with the number of a **telephone information service** for those affected - either directly or indirectly - by domestic violence. Finally, a **poster campaign**, aimed at reinforcing the central themes of the television commercials, was run in approximately 150 sites throughout Central Scotland over a 4 week period from the beginning of August 1994. (A series of stills from the main television commercial and other material relating to the campaign are included at Appendix 1.)

The Scottish Office Central Research Unit was asked to co-ordinate a research-based evaluation of the campaign, the main findings of which are presented in this report. The evaluation had two main elements. First, the Centre for Social Marketing at Strathclyde University was commissioned to undertake a detailed qualitative analysis of the way in which the campaign was received and understood by members of the general public, as well as by those who had been directly affected by domestic violence, either as victims or offenders. This research also examined perceptions of and attitudes towards the subject of domestic violence in general. The second element of the campaign was quantitative and was based on a national survey carried out by System Three Scotland. The main aim of this work was to assess the extent of coverage received by the campaign, although it also included questions focusing on respondents' understanding of the campaign and on attitudes towards domestic violence in general.

The core of this report consists of the qualitative evaluation of the campaign undertaken by the Centre for Social Marketing. In addition, the main findings of the quantitative analysis by System Three Scotland are also included at Appendix 3. Two further appendices provide additional information of relevance to the evaluation. Appendix 4 contains an analysis (by Network Scotland) of calls made to the telephone information line. Finally, Appendix 5 provides information from Scottish Women's Aid about the number of referrals received during the course of the campaign compared with the same period of the previous year.

An executive summary draws together the key points from each element of the evaluation.

EXECUTIVE SUMMARY

1.   THE QUALITATIVE EVALUATION - Centre for Social Marketing

The general public's perceptions of domestic violence

- There was widespread awareness among respondents of the issue of domestic violence though it tended not to be at the forefront of their perceptions of violence in general.

- Perceptions of domestic violence tended to be derived from a mix of 'folk knowledge', direct and indirect experiences, and mass media.

- The issue of domestic violence evoked strong imagery. It was variously perceived as:

    - ongoing, escalating, hidden and malicious
    - incorporating physical but also mental violence
    - typically involving a male perpetrator and female victim
    - potentially involving all social classes, although stereotypical working class images were deep-rooted
    - extensive but difficult to quantify because of its often hidden nature

- A range of factors were seen as likely to contribute to domestic violence at its various stages:

    - *initiation*: alcohol, insecurity, upbringing and low income
    - *continuation*: practical and emotional dependency, age, loss of self esteem and self blame, and fear of potential consequences of leaving the relationship
    - *turning points*: children involved or extreme severe injury

- There was little expectation that habitual perpetrators would reform, though it was felt that there might be potential in the early stages. Empathy with the victims was mixed with incredulity that they remained in such relationships.

- Though domestic violence was generally viewed as unacceptable, in certain circumstances it was less likely to be actively condemned - for example, 'one-off' physical violence as part of the 'normal' conflict within a relationship and mutual, often drunken, public violence. Malicious male violence towards a woman which was ongoing and hidden was much more likely to be condemned.

- Respondents had only limited experience of involvement as outsiders in situations of domestic violence and, while concerned, showed considerable uncertainty about whether, when and how to act. Respondents were, however, clear that help should be directed towards the victim rather than the perpetrator of such violence.

- There was a widespread belief that police and court activity was minimal and that they could and should do more to address the issue of domestic violence.

- It was also felt that any attempt to emphasise the criminality of domestic violence might be undermined by perceived inactivity or ineffectiveness on the part of the courts and the police.

The general public's response to the campaign

The forty second television commercial

- The main television commercial had a high impact and left a strong moral and emotional impression on most respondents. It was vividly recalled and clearly seen to be about domestic violence. Many reported having discussed the campaign with friends or colleagues around the time of the initial screenings.

- It delivered the message that domestic violence is wrong and that perpetrators should face up to their actions, and it aroused emotions of abhorrence and condemnation.

- It was seen as being aimed at two target groups, primarily male perpetrators but also female victims. It was seen to speak directly to perpetrators, encouraging them to examine and to change their behaviour. It was also seen to be indirectly telling female victims that their problem was recognised and encouraging them to seek help. This theme was more enduring because of the impact of the image of the woman's bruised face.

- There were some minor variations in the way the commercial was interpreted, but these did not seem to interfere with the main message and, in some cases, appear to have promoted debate on the subject.

- To some extent, however, the commercial reinforced stereotypical images of domestic violence. There was a focus on physical rather than mental violence and a link with alcohol was implied, which, together with the launch during the Football World Cup, could reinforce an association with working class men.

- The use of visible facial bruising to signify domestic violence was not felt to reflect existing awareness of the wide range of physical and mental abuse experienced by women or the fact that much violence against women would be directed at parts of the body which would not be readily seen by outsiders.

- The 'domestic violence is a crime' message tended not to be well remembered at an unprompted level, though it provided new information to those less well informed. It was also felt that the emphasis on the criminality of domestic violence was unlikely to deter offenders, and many respondents were sceptical about how seriously the police and courts would treat incidents of domestic violence.

- Finally, the commercial was not seen to be speaking directly to the general public but to perpetrators and victims. While the commercial was seen to confirm the seriousness of the problem and to raise awareness of the issue, it was not seen as challenging the public to make any personal contribution nor giving any guidance about what that contribution might be.

The ten second television commercial

- The main strength of the short commercial was that it could potentially add credibility to the campaign as a whole, since it was perceived as offering support which would meet the needs aroused by the forty second commercial.

- However, many failed to recall the ten second commercial, while those who did, did not always link it to the main commercial. As a result its potential to enhance and support the forty second commercial was limited.

- There were also perceived to be some inconsistencies between the tone and message of the forty second commercial which focused on the criminality of domestic violence and the ten second commercial which offered support and help.

- It was felt that the ten second commercial did not give sufficient encouragement to telephone: for example, assurances of confidentiality for both victims and perpetrators were not given.

The telephone service and information pack

- Most respondents expected the freephone telephone service to provide confidential, objective, personal counselling along with practical advice and were surprised and dismayed to learn that the service provided was a recorded message and leaflet request service. It was felt that callers would feel considerably let down by such a service, since it was anticipated that many would be in a state of distress at the time of the call. It was also considered unlikely that they would feel able to leave a message or to make the follow-on calls suggested by the recorded message.

- Respondents were generally dismissive of the information pack, as it was felt that receiving and reading such material undetected would be problematic. It was also felt that non-personal support such as literature would be largely ineffective - though some respondents acknowledged that it might have a limited role to play in supporting face-to-face initiatives. It was felt that the contents of the pack itself were diverse and fragmented, suggesting poor co-ordination and a failure to recognise and address the needs of key caller groups.

'Love and Hate' outdoor poster

- The 'Love and Hate' poster generated considerable awareness. It had high impact and conveyed powerful provocative images in an easily absorbed manner.

- However, the message was ambiguous and some felt it could be counter-productive in that it could support male perpetrators in their behaviour or be felt to be threatening to women, particularly those who had been the victims of domestic violence.

- A further drawback was that it was seen as reinforcing the commonly held stereotype of perpetrators of such violence as working class, 'rough', 'criminal' types.

- In addition, it was not clearly linked to the remainder of The Scottish Office campaign, although it was seen as part of the varied media coverage of the domestic violence issue at the time.

The perpetrators' perspective

- Perpetrators tended to see the campaign as part of a general move towards tackling the issue of domestic violence and creating a climate of intolerance. None, however, were aware of it prompting anyone to comment on or address their own violent behaviour.

- The research suggests that advertising may have an intermediate role to play in both facilitating action among immediate family and friends, and in encouraging those perpetrators *who recognise* that they need support to contact appropriate services. Those who did not acknowledge a problem were unlikely to identify with the campaign

• However, at the moment, the campaign message and tone do not appear to encourage this as the punitive element of the campaign may actively discourage perpetrators from seeking such support. In addition, the support offered was considered inadequate.

• A strategy which offers support to perpetrators appears to be at odds with one which seeks to emphasise the criminal nature of the behaviour and to stimulate a general climate of abhorrence, since the latter approach risks forcing perpetrators further underground and away from any support network.

The victims' perspective

• Victims gave vivid descriptions of their experiences of living with a violent partner. Many of the issues highlighted were also mentioned by the general public, suggesting considerable awareness of the problems faced by victims.

• There was broad support from victims for campaigning on the issue of domestic violence and for The Scottish Office campaign in particular.

• However, there was also some criticism of aspects of the campaign. In particular, it was felt that it did not portray the range of physical, mental and sexual abuse experienced by women. In addition. the extensive bruising on the victim's face was considered to be atypical as it was felt that physical abuse would normally be targeted on the victim's body where it could not be seen by others. Importantly, it was also suggested that the extreme nature of the injuries - and their localised and overtly physical nature - might discourage victims from identifying with the campaign.

• Concern was expressed over the setting of the commercial in a pub, since this was seen to imply that alcohol was the cause of domestic violence when, in reality, violence often occurred without the presence of alcohol.

• Members of the victims' groups were also highly critical of the ten second follow-up commercial and the telephone information line, for similar reasons to those identified by members of the general public. It was also felt that having an information pack sent to the caller might cause considerable practical difficulties or even result in further violence.

• Finally, it was felt that there was a need to address any expectations raised by the campaign through appropriate follow-up and support.

2. THE QUANTITATIVE EVALUATION - System Three Scotland (Appendix 3)

- The initial burst of television activity achieved an exceptionally high level of impact in being recalled spontaneously by more than 8 in 10 survey respondents (81%). Spontaneous recall of television advertising was slightly lower in Stage 2, after intermittent showings of the commercial during the autumn - nevertheless, at 75%, it remained very high.

- When respondents were shown a photo-prompt relating to the forty-second commercial, levels of awareness were even higher - 91% at Stage 1 and 89% at Stage 2. At each stage, at least 82% in all demographic and geographic sub-groups had seen the commercial and, at Stage 2, 97% of 16-24 year olds had done so - a very high figure.

- Almost two-thirds of respondents agreed strongly that the commercial was trying to show that a man who beats his partner can be prosecuted.

- (91%) of respondents agreed that the commercial 'certainly makes you think about domestic violence', but only 30% agreed that it had told them something new.

3. CALLS MADE TO THE DOMESTIC VIOLENCE INFORMATION LINE - Network Scotland (Appendix 4)

- Between 20 June 1994 and 23 December 1994, a total of 13,194 calls were made to the telephone information line.

- These calls led to requests for information packs in 1,139 cases (9%).

- A quarter of the requests for information packs were made by men and three-quarters by women.

4. REFERRALS TO SCOTTISH WOMEN'S AID (Appendix 5)

- Referrals to 14 of the 38 Scottish Women's Aid groups for the years 1993/4 and 1994/5 (the figures for the remaining groups are not, as yet, available) show an increase of 3,382 (47%) over the period during which the domestic violence media campaign was running - a much larger increase than over any previous 12 month period.

- Although it is impossible to establish a direct causal link on the basis of this information, it seems likely that this increase is at least partly due to the campaign.

5.   CONCLUSION

The report identifies the main successful features of the campaign, notably:

- the extent of coverage achieved (roughly 9 in 10 respondents had seen the television campaign)

- the high impact of the campaign (it was vividly recalled by most respondents and many reported having discussed it with friends and colleagues)

- the effective communication of the message that domestic violence should be condemned and that perpetrators should face up to the consequences of their actions

- there was broad support for campaigning on the issue of domestic violence, both from victims and from the public in general.

The research also points to certain weaknesses, and these will be taken into account in planning the next phase of the campaign. For example:

- aspects of both the television commercial and the poster campaign were felt to reinforce stereotypical notions about the nature, incidence and causes of domestic violence

- a strategy which offers support to perpetrators appears to be at odds with one which seeks to emphasise the criminality of domestic violence, since offenders may be discouraged from seeking support

- the information line was widely felt to be inadequate, since it was believed that the television campaign would have set up expectations of a staffed helpline, providing practical and emotional support to victims of domestic violence.

DOMESTIC VIOLENCE MEDIA CAMPAIGN

QUALITATIVE EVALUATION

Susan MacAskill and Douglas Eadie

Centre for Social Marketing
University of Strathclyde

ACKNOWLEDGEMENT

The researchers would like to thank all those who contributed to the project, especially those who related their experiences of abusive relationships.

1.0 INTRODUCTION

1.1 Background

In June 1994, The Scottish Office Home and Health Department (SOHHD) launched a campaign about domestic violence. A mass media campaign was run comprising two television commercials and one poster. In addition, a telephone information service was promoted which provided callers with an information pack on request (Appendix 1).

The aims and targets for the campaign were first, to encourage male perpetrators to think about the implications and consequences of their violent behaviour towards their female partners and, secondly, to foster an atmosphere of public condemnation towards the perpetrators of such violence. Finally, as the programme was developed, a third main target group, victims of domestic violence, was also incorporated.

Two evaluations of the campaign were planned, one quantitative and the other qualitative. The Centre for Social Marketing (CSM) was commissioned to carry out the qualitative element.

The report outlines the research aims and methodology and then describes the main findings. The key areas covered are: the general public's perceptions of domestic violence; their response to the campaign elements and to the campaign as a whole; and the response of the two remaining target groups, namely perpetrators and victims.

1.2 Research aims

Reflecting the aims of the campaign, the research had three main objectives;

To examine the public's:

- perceptions of and attitudes towards domestic violence,

- understanding of the nature and extent of domestic violence,

- comprehension of and response to the media campaign.

It was also intended to interview perpetrators and victims to assess the impact of the campaign on these target groups. Resource limitations meant that this formed a secondary part of the research.

1.3 Method

Qualitative group discussion methods were used. This method involves bringing together, in an informal setting, groups of six or seven respondents who are carefully selected in socio-demographic terms. They are then asked to discuss, in depth, areas of interest, under the direction of a group moderator.

The resulting procedure has many advantages and stimulates a wide review of the issues. Areas are discussed and explored rather than a specific question and answer procedure being adopted. The method allows respondents to select their own priorities in exploring the subject, thereby ensuring the areas covered do not simply reflect the biases of the researcher.

A discussion brief was used to ensure all the areas of interest were covered (Appendix 2).

1.4 Sample

(i)   Primary Sample

The main sample was recruited from the general public. Ten focus group discussions were carried out. The main quota criteria were age, gender, socio-economic group and location.

Gender:	Eight single sex groups were recruited, four male and four female. A further two groups were each made up of four couples who were currently living together.
Age:	The sample was interviewed in two age bands, 20 - 35 year olds and 36 -50 year olds.
Socio-economic group:	Six of the groups were working class (C2DE) and four were middle class (ABC1).
Location:	Six of the groups were carried out in the West of Scotland and four in the East.

All respondents were selected as being or having recently been in a heterosexual relationship for at least six months.

Recruitment and interviewing were carried out in three stages: prior to the campaign, the middle and towards the end of the campaign; in mid-June, early August and early September.

Group	Gender	Age	Socio-economic Group	Location	Timing
1	Female	20 - 35	ABC1	West	Early September
2	Female	20 - 35	C2DE	East	Early August
3	Female	36 - 50	C2DE	West	Mid-June
4	Female	36 - 50	C2DE	West	Early August
5	Male	20 - 35	ABC1	West	Early September
6	Male	20 - 35	C2DE	East	Early August
7	Male	36 - 50	ABC1	East	Early September
8	Male	36 - 50	C2DE	West	Mid-June
9	Mixed	20 - 35	C2DE	West	Early August
10	Mixed	36 - 50	ABC1	East	Early September

(ii)   Secondary Sample

Four focus groups of female victims of violence were interviewed, together with one group of male perpetrators.

1.5 Recruitment

(i)   Primary Sample

Respondents in the primary sample were recruited door-to-door by CSM research consultants using quasi-random selection procedures. Given the sensitive nature of the topic and to satisfy ethical codes of practice, those identified as matching the quota criteria were informed of the topic for discussion and given the opportunity to opt out on those grounds.

(ii)   Secondary Sample

The secondary sample of victims and perpetrators was recruited through support agencies working with those involved in domestic violence, the former through Women's Aid and the latter through the criminal justice system. It should therefore be noted that most of these respondents had been in abusive situations for some time and had not just experienced 'one-off' violence. In addition, many of the victims' sample had been living separately from their violent partners before the launch of the campaign.

2.0 THE GENERAL PUBLIC'S PERCEPTIONS OF DOMESTIC VIOLENCE

This section explores the general public's perceptions of domestic violence, thus setting the context for response to The Scottish Office campaign. Sources of public perceptions are explored (Section 2.1), followed by the scope of those perceptions (Section 2.2), the perceived potential factors in the initiation and continuation of domestic violence (Section 2.3), the acceptability of domestic violence (Section 2.4) and the involvement of others, including the general public and the police (Section 2.5).

2.1 Sources of awareness of domestic violence

Domestic violence did not tend to be spontaneously mentioned by respondents in the context of violence as a whole. However, when prompted, 'domestic violence' was a phrase with which respondents were familiar and there was wide awareness of the issues with some having considerable detailed knowledge of certain aspects.

It was, however, often difficult for respondents to determine from where these opinions derived. Thus there seemed to be considerable general 'folk knowledge' in the community at large rather than specific sources of information. However, three themes did emerge, direct and indirect contact and the mass media which are discussed below.

2.1.1 Direct contact

Few examples of personal experience of what was felt to be domestic violence were raised in the groups. None of the respondents drawn from the general public described themselves as currently being in a physically abusive relationship. One woman described a situation where she had been mentally abused by her partner over a period of time, but that this had now been resolved.

However, it should be noted that the interviews were not intended to elicit information about respondents' own experiences of domestic violence and the setting may not have been conducive to such a discussion.

Isolated examples were given when loss of temper with a partner had erupted into behaviour which was seen to be uncontrolled and relatively serious. Thus a few male respondents described situations where they recalled having 'raised their hand' to a partner. This was deeply regretted afterwards and put down to 'things getting out of hand'. They described the strength of feeling as frightening. Others reported having been on the verge of hitting a partner but had held back, for example, by going out for a drive or a walk.

> "I nearly hit a girlfriend ... and I was really scared at the
> thought of doing it, so I just walked out."
> *(Male, 20 -35 years, ABC1)*

> "Years and years and years ago. My (former) girlfriend was
> going on at me for an hour and a half and I was like that
> 'You better stop ...' and I hit her ... and I felt really bad ...
> 'What have I done?, What have I done?'"
> *(Male, 20 - 35 years, ABC1)*

However, such incidents were described as 'one-off' and not repeated.

More commonly described were occasional episodes of loss of temper in the home which lead to the throwing objects in temper which might or might not actually hit the partner, or slamming doors or drawers shut or shouting at each other. These episodes tended to be trivialised and normalised as part of an ordinary relationship.

> "I lifted a frying pan off the cooker when he was annoying
> me and he ducked and the wall got it, but we were only
> about six months married. He didn't know me then."
> *(Female, 36 - 50 years, C2DE)*

> "My husband put a hole through a door. He's hit a door but
> not me. He's probably done that so he wouldn't hit me."
> *(Female, 36 - 50 years, C2DE)*

Importantly, both the direct and indirect forms of violence reported were not seen as ongoing or malicious and therefore were certainly not seen as evidence of domestic violence or an abusive relationship.

2.1.2   Indirect contact

While accounts of direct personal experience were rare, some descriptions of domestic violence involving others known to respondents were given. These episodes had contributed to their knowledge of domestic violence.

Some respondents were in occupations which brought them into contact with violence between partners; for example, late night bus drivers and taxi drivers who had had to cope with violence and abuse between couples.

However, more respondents tended to have 'heard about' violent relationships rather than seen or witnessed them first hand. In all the groups there were reports of violent situations among people known to the respondents. This was most apparent in the female and older groups. For example, in one group discussion, respondents talked about the following range of indirect experiences; a neighbour's daughter who had come back to live with her mother and who was pursued by her abusive partner, a brother's mother-in-law who had been abused for eighteen years unknown to anyone outside the family, an acquaintance who was beaten regularly, a niece who was beaten by her boyfriend when she was pregnant, a woman who had charged her husband with violence, and a home help working in the home of an abused woman.

Thus there was relatively high awareness of real situations of domestic violence but limited direct experience.

2.1.3   Mass media

A range of mass media were mentioned and this seemed to be a pervasive and extensive source of information about issues around domestic violence. Published media included newspaper reports of cases brought to court and magazines which described case histories. Television programmes were also mentioned and included news items and documentaries, together with drama series and soap operas, such as The Bill, Brookside and Eastenders, which covered the topic in their storylines.

> "You see that on the television that they abuse their wives
> and then say 'Sorry, sorry I didn't mean it,' and they forgive
> them."
> *(Female, 20 - 35 years, C2DE)*

Reporting of The Scottish Office campaign was also mentioned, especially the prior media coverage of the television commercial in the newspapers and the television programmes shown in the week of the launch. Zero Tolerance material was also mentioned, although this campaign was much more prominent in the East where exposure had been more extensive and prolonged.

2.2 Perceptions of domestic violence

The phrase 'domestic violence' conjured up a variety of images which are discussed below in terms of; general images of domestic violence (Section 2.2.1), perceived gender of those immediately involved (Section 2.2.2), perceived social class of those immediately involved (Section 2.2.3) and perceived prevalence (Section 2.2.4).

2.2.1 General images of domestic violence

Domestic violence was viewed primarily (but not exclusively) as <u>physical</u> violence. However, respondents, especially women, recognised that it did not always involve 'straightforward' hitting. This is illustrated in this series of comments from respondents in one group.

> "There's a whole big file of things actually encompassed in
> the term domestic violence ..."
> "... punching and hitting ..."
> "... pushed against a wall ..."
> "... slapped in the face ..."
> "... tea or coffee poured over them ..."
> "... taking money ..."
> "... not allowing them to work."
> *(Females, 20 - 35 years, ABC1)*

Mental violence was also identified as indicated in the latter two quotes above. This was not as prominent in respondents' minds as physical violence; however it was seen to be equally if not more harmful and to have more enduring effects.

> "I think it's a mental thing. If a man tells you you are
> rubbish then you think you are rubbish. You can't get on
> with your life."
> *(Female, 20 - 35 years, C2DE)*

> "It doesn't have to be physical, does it? I mean violence can
> be verbal ... but that can be as bad as physically hitting."
> *(Male, 36 - 50 years, ABC1)*

Interestingly, sexual violence was rarely mentioned in the general public groups, although it was seen as important to many in the victim groups (see Section 5.1).

Domestic violence was seen as distinct from the tensions, disputes and, sometimes, physical fights which respondents had described as a 'normal' part of living together with a partner, as discussed in Section 2.1.1. It was considered to be ongoing, although not always regular, and to escalate. Thus once it had started it was felt that perpetrators would feel that they could *'get away with it'* and that it would gradually become more frequent and more malicious. In addition, it was felt that it usually occurred within the home and was therefore hidden from society at large.

The descriptions given by the general public showed a striking consistency with experiences reported by victims (see Section 5.1) although at a relatively superficial level. However, although respondents had some conception of what living in a violent situation could be like, it was felt that only experience could enable one to relate to the personal horror.

"No one can imagine what it's like living with a violent
partner unless it's happening to them."
(Female, 36 - 50 years, C2DE)

2.2.2 Perceived gender of those immediately involved

Domestic violence was seen primarily to involve men being violent or abusive to women and was often referred to as 'wife beating', particularly by males. Male violence was therefore the underlying assumption during the discussions. However, it was also believed that women could be violent towards male partners.

"You hear a lot more on the television about women abusing
men than you used to."
(Female, 20 - 35 years, C2DE)

This was commented on in all the groups but knowledge was much more vague. Female violence was usually raised in the context of discussing media coverage of violence in general and the Zero Tolerance campaign in particular. Concern was expressed that campaigning risked being unbalanced by failing to recognise male victims and some respondents, especially males, appeared to raise the issue of female violence to diminish the importance of male violence. However, the discussion usually concluded with agreement that, since male violence was felt to be more widespread, targeting this issue was justified.

2.2.3 Perceived social class of those immediately involved

Respondents frequently made the point that domestic violence could involve people from all walks of life, in any sort of work and from any kind of background. Thus, at one level, it was seen as non-class specific.

"All people from the highest in the land down."
(Female, 36 - 50 years, C2DE)

However, as the discussions progressed, spontaneous associations and the language used revealed an underlying tendency to associate domestic violence with a working class, low income scenario. Thus strongly stereotyped imagery emerged, although there was also some recognition that these were indeed stereotypes. Thus individual respondents could cite both the working class and non class-specific scenario during the course of the discussions.

Two typical images were evoked:

- The most common image evoked was of an insecure male, recently unemployed, in debt, the wife as the main breadwinner and living in a council housing scheme. He drinks heavily and drink gives him confidence. He is verbally and physically abusive, especially when drunk, and undermines his wife's self esteem. He is apologetic the next day, promises *'it won't happen'* again and is forgiven. However, these violent incidents continue although he may be remorseful and forgiven each time.

    "I think it's more in the deprived areas because you have the
    tension of the poverty trap that you are in and then you

obviously get friction between the man and his wife and it
just boils up more.
(Male, 36 - 50 years, ABC1)

"I think there's a lot of tension in the house, if they are not
working and they are in the house all day long and they are
cracking up because they haven't got any money, and
they've not got any work."
(Female, 36 - 50 years, C2DE)

- A second image, although less prevalent, was of mutual violence with the wife *'giving as good as she gets'*. Again, from a working class background, they are both heavy drinkers and unconcerned about airing their problems in public, often outside a pub or in the street. They have a reputation for such fights in their community and may be members of families notorious for this type of behaviour. They are seen to depend on the mutual violence and abuse - it's *'how they live'*.

This association of domestic violence with working class imagery tended to be rationalised by respondents in one of two ways: either it was attributed to limited publicity about violence in middle class families or it might be argued that there was actually less violence in such families, perhaps because of fewer financial pressures and a less stressful living environment.

"If you had a comfier lifestyle, there's still beatings that go
on but there isn't as many things that will be a flashpoint,
like you can't buy anything for the kids."
(Male, 36 - 50 years, ABC1)

"I think perhaps middle and upper class, they wouldn't tell
anybody if it was happening ... because it's not the done
thing."
(Male, 36 - 50 years, ABC1)

2.2.4 Perceived prevalence of domestic violence

The extent of domestic violence was felt to be considerable. However, because it was seen to occur in the privacy of the home, with each partner having their own reasons for maintaining secrecy, it was believed that the real level is underestimated.

"There must be a lot of people where a lot goes on behind
closed doors. I haven't got a clue. Maybe there are people
hiding it."
(Female, 20 - 35 years, C2DE)

"You always know someone who is very nervous when her
husband comes in."
(Female, 36 - 50 years, C2DE)

It was frequently stated that domestic violence was increasing in prevalence although not necessarily increasing in terms of the severity of the abuse.

"You read a lot more about it in the papers, don't you? It's
happening a lot more now."
(Female, 36 - 50 years, C2DE)

However, it was also argued that increased publicity about domestic violence and increased reporting of incidents may reflect a growing media interest rather than an actual increase in violent behaviour.

2.3 Perceived potential factors in the initiation and continuation of domestic violence

Respondents were able to identify a range of factors in the initiation and continuation of domestic violence (Section 2.3.1 and Section 2.3.2) which are discussed below, together with perceptions of 'turning points,' which may lead the victim to take steps to end the relationship (Section 2.3.3)

2.3.1 Initiation of domestic violence

Four recurring themes emerged as initial causes of domestic violence: drunkenness, personality, 'upbringing' and unemployment.

Drink and drunkenness were frequently mentioned in relation to domestic violence. Alcohol was seen to reduce inhibitions and the ability to behave rationally, although respondents in the victims' groups were concerned that it was sometimes used as an excuse for violence.

> "It gives you security to have a drink, it gives you
> confidence, you can get away with it."
> *(Female, 20 - 35 years, C2DE)*

In addition, many respondents, especially women, associated domestic violence with insecurity in the male perpetrator's personality. It was argued that a violent man may have an unreasonable need to appear 'macho' and may often be possessive and jealous of his wife.

> "If you get one of those insecure guys. You could get the
> guy saying to the woman putting her make up on 'Where are
> you going? What are you looking so happy for?'"
> *(Female, 20 - 35 years, C2DE)*

> "You can have a man who is a bit insecure and then he gets
> made redundant and his wife is still working. If there is a
> wee bit of a personality problem anyway, things can escalate
> from there."
> *(Female, 20 - 35 years, C2DE)*

Some mentioned the need to have power over another individual, an issue also raised in the victims' groups (see Section 5.1).

'Upbringing' was also seen as an important factor affecting victims and perpetrators. Some respondents expressed the view that for those men who had been brought up in a violent home, violence could be the learned response to disagreement. Others, however, felt that this process was not inevitable, and that those brought up in a violent home might develop the determination not to behave similarly.

'Upbringing' was also felt by some to affect women, where it was argued a victim may learn to accept violence as part of a normal relationship.

> "Maybe her parents were doing that sort of thing and they'll
> just accept the way things are ... because the parents had it,
> the grandparents had it."
> *(Male, 36 - 50 years, ABC1)*

> "They see their parents doing it and it's handed down and they think it's okay."
> *(Female, 36 - 50 years, ABC1)*

Finally, unemployment and low income were also seen by many respondents as linked with domestic violence. It was perceived that these circumstances could lead to considerable stress, both financial and from spending time together in the confines of the home (see Section 2.2.3).

2.3.2 Continuation of domestic violence

It was widely believed that if an incident of domestic violence had occurred and the victim made excuses and accepted the situation the violence was likely to be repeated and to increase in severity, perhaps with children eventually being abused.

> "I'm a firm believer of once they do it, they always do it."
> *(Female, 36 - 50 years, C2DE)*

> "It's the security, it's the comfort, it's probably they're too terrified to leave or they are always hoping the next time it won't happen. You know, 'sorry,' then it happens (again)."
> *(Male, 36 - 50 years, ABC1)*

The overwhelming expectation of ending the situation was for the woman to leave the relationship rather than an expectation for the man to reform.

Respondents varied in their reaction to individuals remaining in a situation where there were continuing episodes of violence. Thus, on the one hand, many were incredulous that women put up with the situation and remained with their partner.

> "I would never take that ... if a man hit me once that would be the last."
> *(Female, 36 - 50 years, C2DE)*

> "For me, I just cannot imagine living with someone who hit me. It's beyond my comprehension ... If you've never experienced it. I don't think you can imagine how you can do it. But obviously they do."
> *(Female, Mixed Group, 36 - 50 years, ABC1)*

> "My neighbour's sister, her husband set fire to the family room. He actually went to prison and they've made contact again. How thick is that? ... I just find it unbelievable."
> *(Female, 20 - 35 years, C2DE)*

> "You hear about the wives who get battered and you say 'Why do they stay?'"
> *(Male, 36 - 50 years, ABC1)*

On the other hand there was considerable understanding, particularly among women, about why such a situation could continue. A range of factors were considered important which are discussed below. These showed considerable understanding of the female victim's plight and also fitted with victims' analyses of why they remained in the relationship. Practical considerations were seen to be important particularly if children were involved. However these were also underlying emotional considerations. These are discussed below.

The problem of alternative accommodation was frequently raised, as the victim was usually the

11

one who had to leave the family home. It was believed immediate alternatives would be hard to find, especially if a woman had taken her children with her. Emergency provision was anticipated to be crowded and substandard.

> "I thought, 'stupid bitch, why don't you just leave,' but I know how difficult it is to leave, to uproot themselves and leave their house. Take two or four kids with them."
> *(Female, 20 - 35 years, C2DE)*

> "They take it as long as the kids are getting looked after and they've got a roof over their head."
> *(Male, 36 - 50 years, ABC1)*

> "It's hard to get a house. They've got a house with a mortgage, they've got to stay with it ... If the women is in the red then she can't get another house because she is in arrears."
> *(Female, 20 - 35 years, C2DE)*

In addition, the victim was often felt to be financially dependent on her partner, either because she was not working herself or because her partner had assumed control of her income. This was linked with emotional dependence because her self-confidence was seen as likely to be diminished, resulting in feelings of inadequacy in finding employment or tackling the intricacies of the state benefit system.

It was frequently felt that younger women would be less accepting of violence and that they would be more independent of mind and, in a practical sense, more likely to have their own employment and personal income.

> "I think it's different now. More young women are outspoken, whereas before, women, just like everything else, they cooried in and got on with it."
> *(Female, 36 - 50 years, C2DE)*

However, it was also recognised that emotional ties could remain strong for both younger and older women, in the early stages at least, and a loving relationship could be re-established in between abuse. In addition, many respondents felt that while there were more refuges and support agencies than before and that marriage break-up was more acceptable socially, it would still be difficult to end a relationship.

> "They say it's easier now to walk out on a marriage but I don't think for a moment that it is."
> *(Female, 36 - 50 years, C2DE)*

> "But on top of the violence she might still love him."
> *(Male, 36 - 50 years, ABC1)*

Importantly many anticipated the victim blaming herself for the relationship going wrong, often reinforced in this by her partner. Thus it was anticipated that the victim would feel that it was her responsibility, rather than her partner's, to resolve the situation. Self-blame and embarrassment would make it difficult to obtain support by confiding in family or friends or risking publicity in the press or the courts.

> "A lot of women take it on themselves and they feel guilty. Something out of their control, they don't discuss it."
> *(Female, 36 - 50 years, C2DE)*

12

"I think unfortunately the victims tend to think that they are
at fault in some way. They can talk themselves into, 'I must
have antagonised him' or something like that."
(Male, 36 - 50 years, ABC1)

"Ashamed and embarrassed. A lot of women, that's how
they keep quiet."
(Female, 36 - 50 years, C2DE)

In addition, many believed victims would feel there were benefits to the children in staying in a two parent family despite the violence. However, two female respondents who had been brought up in violent households both felt that their mother should have left their father.

"My mother stuck with him ... which was totally wrong.
All of our lives were miserable. She should have done it
(left) when we were all wee."
(Female, 36 - 50 years, C2DE)

Other consequences were also anticipated. For example, it was felt that women feared their children would be taken into care if they made the violence public. In addition, many felt that there would be fears that partners would follow victims after they had left home and continue to be violent, often despite court interdicts. It was widely believed that the police or courts were unable to provide sufficient protection (see Section 2.5.3).

2.3.3 Potential turning points

It was believed that some women endured these situations, while others reached a turning point when they would seek help and advice and take steps to end the relationship. Respondents identified possible turning points as the involvement of children, either as witnesses or victims of violence, or an extreme episode of violence which was beyond that previously tolerated.

"From what I've read, a lot of wives will stay. They'll
suffer being battered as long as they don't touch the kids."
(Male, 36 - 50 years, ABC1)

"(My sister) was so frightened, she just had to run."
(Female, 36 - 50 years, C2DE)

These were similar reasons to those given by the victims themselves (see Section 5.1).

2.3.4 Overview

The discussions indicated there was a general awareness and understanding of the problems experienced by victims while some had detailed knowledge of specific aspects, primarily from indirect experience.

Importantly the need for the victim to leave the situation was the main focus of discussion. There was little consideration of the man stopping the abuse or leaving which perhaps indicated a predisposition towards victim blaming, albeit mixed with sympathy for the victim. While demonstrating an understanding of the woman's predicament, respondents tended to remain incredulous as to the victim's decision to stay in the relationship.

2.4 Acceptability of domestic violence

The research sought to explore whether and how the acceptability of domestic violence varied according to circumstance.

When discussing violence in general, it was viewed by all respondents as unacceptable. Respondents were reluctant to consider themselves as violent and condemned perpetrators of violence. However, there were some aspects of violence which were less readily condemned. Where the violence only involved those immediately concerned and did not affect others, was not seen as worth attention by the police and did not result in lasting damage apparent to outsiders, then it would be relatively more acceptable. In the same way, variations in acceptability of violence appeared to extend to the domestic situation.

When asked directly, the unanimous response was that domestic violence was completely unacceptable. This was expressed as *"I wouldn't do it"* primarily by men or as *"they shouldn't do it"* by women. Both men and women felt that the victim should not accept such violence.

However, there were some indications that, in certain situations, domestic violence would be less likely to arouse concern. This was more apparent in the earlier stages of the discussion before the specific focus on domestic violence had become apparent.

Thus, during indirect questioning respondents, especially older men, often demonstrated some degree of acceptance of domestic violence, *'it's a personal thing between husband and wife''*. Others provided tacit approval by treating it with flippant comments and jokes. In some isolated instances stronger prejudices existed (*they get what they deserve'*), for example, if the female partner had been unfaithful or *'nagged the face off him'* or overspent on the family budget. This was unlike child abuse which had <u>no</u> support at any level.

More detailed discussion revealed that attitudes could shift, depending upon circumstance. Thus, respondents found it difficult to maintain the stance that all domestic violence is unacceptable. For example, it was felt that alcohol seemed to be used in some circumstances as an excuse for violence. It appeared that society, as well as the victim and perpetrator, could condone excesses in behaviour where they could be linked to drinking, provided there was not repeated violent behaviour.

Another example is the scenario described from personal experience, namely the occasional 'bad patch' when an argument had got out of hand, resulting in a lot of shouting, throwing of objects or the raising of a hand (see Section 2.1). In such a scenario the woman is equally as capable as the man of perpetrating a violent act.

> "I had a blazing row with my wife when I was unemployed - as a sort of release of tension. She hit me a couple of times but I wouldn't let myself vice versa and she felt really bad for that ... You know that's it, you've had your one and that's it and never again but there's a certain tolerance of certain things."
> *(Male, 36 - 50 years, ABC1)*

Although unpleasant, such incidents were not spontaneously defined as 'domestic violence', largely because they were one-off and not malicious and so were not actively condemned.

> "If it occurs regularly (violence), that's when it starts to bubble."
> *(Male, 36 - 50 years, ABC1)*

"When it goes over a blind rage ... starts becoming harmful."
(Female, 20 - 35 years, C2DE)

Significantly the message that 'you only have to hit your partner once to commit a crime', was therefore not related by respondents to this area of personal experience.

"The police are really busy and if you phoned up saying he slapped you the police are going to be really pleased (sarcastic)."
(Female, 20 - 35 years, C2DE)

Alternatively, respondents also visualised habitual violence, where patterns of behaviour have been established over many years, often where both partners, usually both drunk, abused each other (see Section 2.2.3). In these situations, the response elicited again tended to be - *'it's up to them'*, *'they've got themselves caught in a rut'* and *'they need to sort it out themselves'* and intervention would be unlikely.

Such scenarios represented areas where acceptance tended to be higher. More unacceptable, and where most condemnation was focused, was the grey area of violence experienced by others which was likely to take place behind closed doors. This was the area where there was greatest uncertainty and least experience. As a result, many found it difficult to determine whether or how to intervene. Despite this, there was often a desire or an expressed need to act. This mismatch between desire to act and inability to determine the course of action to take often led to a sense of powerlessness and perhaps characterises the existing tolerance surrounding the problem.

2.5 Involvement of others

This section explores respondents attitudes towards the concept of third parties intervening in a violent domestic situation. As stated in the introduction, the campaign aimed to foster an atmosphere of public condemnation of domestic violence, hence it was of interest to explore the public's feelings about personal intervention in a situation: whether they felt they should act, whether they would feel able to act; what might hold them back; and the potential for involving outside support agencies. Given the focus of the main forty second television commercial on the criminality of domestic violence, the public's perceptions of police and court involvement in this area of crime were also of interest.

The perceived roles of three main groups were examined; the general public (Section 2.5.1), support agencies (Section 2.5.2) and the police and judiciary (Section 2.5.3).

2.5.1 Involvement of the general public

Potential interventions by the general public were most often visualised as being out of concern for the victim rather than the perpetrator. A very few respondents had intervened in a domestic dispute. This had been in a variety of ways, for example, telephoning the police during an incident, talking to either the victim or perpetrator or providing a place of safety for the victim.

Respondents felt that, although there was a potential role for the public to intervene in a violent domestic situation in order to prevent a crisis or offer support, several factors made this sort of lay intervention problematic. A range of considerations for and against intervention were described by respondents and are illustrated in this series of quotes taken from one of the groups.

"If it was kids ..."
"If I felt capable ..."
"If I could I would ..."
"When you know people ..."
"If you jump in, they could mess you up."
(Females, 20 - 35 years, C2DE)

Thus there would be a protracted decision-making process undertaken, considering when, whether and how to intervene. The factors which were thought might be taken into account are discussed below.

(i)   Perceived situations when the public might intervene

Respondents described a range of circumstances where intervention might take place, which formed a background to the actual decision regarding whether or not to intervene.

First, some respondents visualised intervening while a violent act was actually taking place while others visualised talking to the perpetrator or the victim after the event. The former intervention was primarily visualised by men and the latter was more likely to be described by women.

"Me and the boy across the landing got a hold of the boy and said to him, 'You better get your act together or we are going to do something about it.'"
(Male, 36 - 50 years, C2DE)

"You might try and help, try and give them advice or try and get them help if they couldn't do it for themselves."
(Female, 20 - 35 years, C2DE)

Secondly, if an intervention was considered after a period of violence, respondents described the dilemma of deciding between, on the one hand, initiating the contact and raising the issue personally, such as asking a woman if there was a problem, or on the other hand, waiting to receive a plea for help.

"I'd rather she ended up no' speaking to me and saying something to her, than her end up getting killed, than then thinking that I should have said something."
(Female, 36 - 50 years, C2DE)

"If I was getting battered I would need someone else to say it first or if you noticed a bruise or anything ... 'I walked into a door,' ... Is she wanting me to see this?"
(Female, 36 - 50 years, C2DE)

"They would need to approach me."
(Female, 36 - 50 years, C2DE)

Finally, respondents also visualised having to decide whether to intervene personally or whether to call in other agencies such as the police or social workers.

(ii)   Factors making involvement more or less likely

A variety of factors were discussed which were seen as making personal involvement more or less likely. These were not seen in isolation but were felt to interact and combine to tip the balance for or against action.

16

<u>Degree of certainty about the events</u>

The visibility of the situation and corresponding degree of certainty as to whether abuse was taking place was significant. Thus, where the violent act took place behind closed doors, there was less certainty. Respondents were reluctant to act for fear of misinterpreting the situation. This problem was compounded by both partners maintaining secrecy.

> "You just suspect, because you have seen something that just isn't right. You know, that's where it becomes very difficult. You could blow your whole credibility in the air if you're wrong, couldn't you?"
> *(Male, Mixed Group, 36 - 50 years, ABC1)*

Intervention was considered more likely where assistance was actually requested, from either victim or perpetrator as opposed to the respondent having to, first, decide whether a problem existed and secondly, decide whether outside input would be welcomed or rejected.

> "I think they would need to approach me and say, 'Look this (abuse), this is happening.'"
> *(Female, 36 - 50 years, C2DE)*

<u>Uncertainty about how to act</u>

Importantly, even if they were concerned, many respondents were often uncertain about the course of action they might take and what to do or say. This confusion often acted as a deterrent to getting involved.

> "I think some people would like to do something but don't know what to do."
> *(Male, 20 - 35 years, ABC1)*

> "I wouldn't know what kind of advice I could give to someone ..."
> "You don't know if you're giving the right advice ..."
> "You'd probably use your common sense."
> *(Females, 36 - 50 years, C2DE)*

Some also feared that their actions might prove counter-productive, leading to further abuse.

<u>Expectation of a successful outcome</u>

Respondents often held the view that women in abusive relationships frequently resumed the relationship after a violent episode. This, many argued, acted as a disincentive to intervene.

> "I think there's no way of interfering. She's just going to go back to him anyway. He's not going to stop."
> *(Female, Mixed Group, 36 - 50 years, ABC1)*

> "I think it is hard to get involved with couples because they end up getting back together again."
> *(Female, 20 - 35 years, C2DE)*

In addition, failure to make the intended impact, could mean people were reluctant to make any further efforts and also led to frustration for those trying to offer support. Respondents described personal experiences of this situation.

> "It's one of those things where you want to yell or scream at

them, 'Why don't you do something about it?' and they say
'But I can't.'"
> *(Female, 20 - 35 years, ABC1)*

"I'd phoned the police, they did turn up. I mean I was
somewhat surprised they did turn up and dealt with it.
Actually he was dragged downstairs with the police and she
came screaming out the door, 'Don't hit him, don't hit
him.'"
> *(Male, Mixed Group, 36 - 50 years, ABC1)*

Perceived repercussions from intervening

Respondents expressed concern that an intervention might have repercussions both to
themselves and their family. In particular, there was felt to be a risk of being attacked by either
the perpetrator or the victim or both.

> "Depends how much you want to intrude in people's lives.
> The first couple of times (neighbours fighting) I tried to go
> along and have a chat to the guy and I was told to basically
> mind my f... business or it would be me next. Then you
> have your family saying, 'Don't get involved, you know.
> What happens, next time if he comes to the door with a knife
> or something?'"
> *(Male, 36 - 50 years, ABC1)*

> "I saw a bloke was going to slap his female partner about
> and actually hit her. Another guy had actually gone to break
> it up and the woman had actually gone for the guy for
> breaking it up ... It's her man and it's their wee life."
> *(Female, 20 - 35 years, C2DE)*

> "I made the mistake of getting involved in it once and I
> won't do it again. The two of them actually turned on me."
> *(Male, 36 - 50 years, C2DE)*

Thus involvement was considered more likely if in a safe situation. For example, in a pub
where one was known and where others would support the action.

Other perceived risks included losing contact with the victim, damaging an existing friendship
or being left in a difficult situation if the couple subsequently got back together again. Active
involvement had long term implications and it was not the type of crime one could walk away
from having become involved.

If someone was felt to be being seriously injured or harmed or their life appeared to be in
danger, intervention was considered more likely.

> "If they were slapping each other about I wouldn't bother
> but obviously if he was killing her you would have to do
> something."
> *(Male, 36 - 50 years, C2DE)*

Similarly, if others were involved, especially children, respondents claimed that they were
more likely to intervene.

> "Everybody is more likely to step in if it was a child that was
> being abused rather than an adult."
> *(Female, Mixed Group, 36 - 50 years, ABC1)*

Personal motives were also significant for some, such as the inconvenience caused by the noise from the fighting. Where the abuse was less personally disruptive, some respondents indicated that they would be less inclined to intervene.

> "If the man and woman are fighting next door constantly, the only thing that is going to annoy me is the noise. Apart from that it is none of my business."
> *(Male, 36 - 50 years, C2DE)*

Familiarity with the victim or perpetrator

Familiarity with the people concerned, where they are friends or family, was claimed to increase the likelihood of getting involved.

> "If it was someone I know ... someone in the family, I'd interfere."
> *(Female, 36 - 50 years, C2DE)*

This, however, did not always accord with the experiences related by the victims themselves, some of whom were rejected by their families (see Section 5.1).

Respect for personal privacy

Respect for personal privacy was also an issue frequently raised. There was a tendency to take the view that domestic violence was a matter for husband and wife, especially among older and male respondents and that outsiders should not interfere.

> "If I am having an argument with my wife the last thing I want is someone poking their nose into my affairs."
> *(Male, 36 - 50 years, C2DE)*

(iii)   Potential help and advice given

Many respondents were uncertain about how to help in specific situations, although they had some general ideas. Importantly, the giving of help and advice was seen primarily in terms of support for the victims rather than the perpetrator and in circumstances outwith a violent episode.

The initial advice offered was likely to be short and perhaps simplistic, *"get out."* As previously discussed, despite showing understanding of why women do stay within an abusive relationship, respondents found it difficult to empathise with this decision to remain (see Section 2.3).

It was also felt that providing a 'listening ear' could in some instances useful. This, it was agreed, gave the victim an opportunity to talk through her worries and problems and, in some instances, allowed her to come to her own conclusions about the best course of action.

> "You just have to have been there - just to sit and listen. There is no' really a lot you can do."
> *(Female, 36 - 50, C2DE)*

> "I would sit and try to talk to them about it. Find out if I could help, give them some advice."
> *(Female, 36 - 50 years, C2DE)*

> "We can only do so much as it is as outsiders looking in. If

the woman from whatever the actual abuse is for, sexual or
violent, they don't feel comfortable about coming out and
finding someone to talk to."
(Male, Mixed Group, 36 - 50 years, ABC1)

A number of respondents claimed that they would suggest to the victim that she approach the support services for advice, mentioning those discussed below (see Section 2.5.2). Younger respondents were more confident about offering this type of advice, often claiming that appropriate services could be easily identified via the telephone directory or the Citizens Advice Bureau. Older respondents were more wary of these services and of the potential problems of involvement. Bringing in the police was considered a more likely course of action when a violent act was actually taking place.

(v)   Overview

Overall then, there was considerable confusion and uncertainty on the part of the general public about how to deal with instances of domestic violence. Considerable soul-searching was likely to ensue before intervening. Concerns were expressed over: if and when to get involved; what was the most useful course of action; and what the likely consequences were. Some were more reluctant than others to intervene.

Victims' accounts of their own experiences tended to support respondents' perceptions. They had had a mixed response when they had needed help and support (see Section 5.1.3). However, they were uncertain about recommending strategies for effective support from the public. It was felt that different interventions would be appropriate in different situations and there was a risk that attempts to help might be ineffective or counter-productive.

2.5.2 Involvement of support agencies

A range of support agencies that victims might approach were identified by the respondents. These included Women's Aid, Social Work Departments, Relate, the Citizens Advice Bureau and general practitioners. There was no mention by respondents of services where male perpetrators could seek help, which perhaps reflects the underlying belief that it was up to the victim to take action.

Some respondents, especially those from the younger age groups, felt that there were many potential sources of help. However, older respondents were less inclined to encourage outside help.

Reluctance on the part of the victim to approach agencies for help was perceived to be related to a belief that often outsiders were unable to deal effectively with the problem, together with a feeling of personal responsibility to resolve the situation and shame and embarrassment about the situation. Others felt, however, that there could be value in involving an outside agency. The dilemma is shown in these sequential comments taken from one group discussion.

"If you can't sort it out for yourself what good is it going to
do talking to strangers about it ..."
"I think I could talk to a stranger better, someone who isn't
involved. I'd be less embarrassed, they don't know us."
(Females, 36 - 50 years, C2DE)

In addition, it was anticipated that approaching outside agencies could result in unwanted repercussions, such as involvement by the courts and social services, the potential break up of the family and the threat of further violence by the perpetrator. It was, therefore, felt by many that it would require considerable courage for the victim to seek help. Thus it was concluded that what victims required was, in the first instance, a confidential advice service to discuss their options and arrive at an informed decision about their best course of action given their personal circumstances.

(i)   Women's Aid

Women's Aid was frequently mentioned in the general public groups. It was referred to directly by name or indirectly by reference to refuges.

> "You go to these homes for battered wives for about six weeks and after that you have to find some other accommodation."
> *(Female, 20 - 35 years, C2DE)*

Although many were aware of the organisation, few had a detailed knowledge of the service and support it offered. A few respondents knew women who had found it beneficial and sympathetic to their situation, but there was a widespread belief that it was for women who were frequently and severely physically abused, rather than supporting victims of all types of domestic violence.

(ii)   Social Work Services

Social work services, although frequently mentioned, were seen as more necessary and active where children were involved and where re-housing was a problem. Respondents were often reluctant to involve such services themselves. There was a general feeling that social workers *"take too much on themselves"* and might perhaps enlarge the problem and therefore many respondents would be reluctant to suggest that victims approach social work services. Foremost was the perceived risk that children could be taken into care in such situations.

(iii)   Relate

This agency was generally referred to as Marriage Guidance. It was believed to deal with problems associated with the general breakdown in a relationship rather than domestic violence specifically. It was therefore assumed to be of limited help where the victim was physically at risk. In practical terms it was believed there would be long delays for appointments which would be inappropriate when the victim and her family were in need of more immediate and substantive forms of support.

(iv)   Citizens Advice Bureau

The Citizens Advice Bureau was mentioned more frequently by younger respondents. It was seen as a primary source of advice on contacting relevant support agencies.

(v)   General Practitioners

Family doctors were also mentioned as a potential source of advice and support, since it was anticipated that abused women would approach them for medical attention. However, it was believed that it would be difficult for victims to confess the cause of their injuries. Victims themselves volunteered this view, citing instances where they had hidden the reason from their doctor (see Section 5.1.2).

2.5.3 Involvement of the Police and Judiciary

This section examines the sources influencing respondents' perceptions of the police and the courts in respect to domestic violence, and then examines their perceptions in terms of their level and nature of involvement and the perceived consequences for the victim.

(i) Sources influencing perceptions of the police and judiciary

Respondents held strong opinions about the criminal justice system and its role in tackling domestic violence. However, they found it difficult to identify what influenced these perceptions. Notably, very few said they had direct personal experience of the legal system in this area.

There was a similar pattern to that described in Section 2.1. In the same way, there appeared to be an underlying 'folk knowledge' of this issue with generally negative impressions. The phrase, *"it's a domestic"*, was readily used in this area of discussion, conveying a belief that the police and courts tended not to take a proactive stance in this area of violence. However, there were also more positive impressions, as discussed in detail below. Significantly, in the few instances where respondents had indirect experience of the system, some cases were described where the police had been helpful and the system as a whole had been supportive.

Above and beyond direct experience, the main factor that appeared to influence perceptions was the mass media. This included television programmes, both documentaries and dramas and particularly soap operas like Brookside and Eastenders and series, such as The Bill and Casualty. Newspapers were also mentioned, referring to reports of court cases and sentencing.

Finally, The Scottish Office campaign was also referred to in this context in the later discussion groups. Some respondents who described domestic violence as a crime, recalled that they had learnt this from the main forty second television commercial.

(ii) The police - perceived nature and levels of involvement

Respondents described three levels of perceived police involvement in domestic violence.

First, there was isolated awareness of what was seen to be appropriate action by the police. This was usually derived from cases personally known to the respondents. The scenario described was of the police arriving quickly at the scene, taking the man away and, ideally, charging him, and giving support to the woman victim by providing a woman police constable who could offer advice and referring the victim to support agencies such as Women's Aid.

Secondly, there existed a more general awareness that the police were active to some extent. For example, many thought officers might attend the scene and attempt to calm the man down or take him away overnight if their efforts proved fruitless.

> "The woman left her husband and she went back to stay with
> her mum and he came down and put their door through and
> they phoned the police ... I know the police came straight
> away."
> *(Female, 36 - 50 years, C2DE)*

Thirdly, the predominant belief was that the police were not active, only responding or reporting the incident when and if there was severe physical injury. This opinion was more prevalent among older respondents. It was believed that the police would not become involved in instances of 'just a slap' or 'one hit' and in incidents of mental cruelty.

"I think it's a crying shame. The police, when they hear
that's what it is, they take nothing to do with it."
(Female, 36 - 50 years, C2DE)

"From what I know about police, they tend to keep away
from domestic situations."
(Male, 36 - 50 years, ABC1)

Attitudes to these underlying perceptions of police activity tended to shift from criticism, *"the police don't do anything"*, to sympathy, *"they can't do anything"*, both within the groups and among individuals. At a critical level it was felt that the police 'ought to do something', and that they seemed uncaring and ineffective. It was also hoped that this situation would improve now that domestic violence had been highlighted as a crime. On the other hand, at a sympathetic level, many recognised that, because domestic violence was normally within the privacy of the home, it would be difficult for the police to take effective action without the support of the victim and a witness. A common scenario described in most groups was of the police being called to the scene and then the victim regretting the action, either through fear of reprisal from their partner or because the relationship was re-established. In light of this, it was felt the police would be reluctant to do the necessary paperwork when there was a strong likelihood that the case would be dropped.

"I don't blame them for being totally cheesed off because if
you get there and it's okay if you are going to charge
somebody, but if you get there and it has all changed and
they don't want them charged, what is the point? Although
people criticise the police I can see why their attitude is such
that they can't be bothered."
(Female, 20 - 35 years, C2DE)

It was also felt that it was difficult for the police to enforce separation orders and interdicts.

These perceptions often reflected the victims' experiences (see Section 5.1.3). Some described feeling abandoned by the police, even in recent years, while others reported that they had found the police helpful - *"the police are better these days."* It appeared that the quality of the service was patchy and experiences were varied. In addition, victims confirmed that in the past it had not been unusual for them to call out the police and then go back to their partner afterwards.

Finally, the police service's counselling role and links with the social services was not widely recognised by the public.

(iii) *Perceived court activity*

Attitudes to the courts were less fluid than those to the police and generally tended to be more critical. It was widely believed that few cases of domestic violence reached court. When they did reach the courts it was felt a conviction was unlikely as in many instances proof would be difficult, or it was felt that the punishment would be minimal, with only small fines or short periods of imprisonment. A view frequently voiced was that there should be more severe sentencing.

"I think the law is terrible ... too lenient on them ... you
know, three months, six months ... for black eyes and
everything. The judge doesn't know what that woman's
been through."
(Female, 36 - 50 years, C2DE)

Respondents' perceptions of the punishments given compared unfavourably with more serious sentencing for crimes such as grievous bodily harm and robbery. It was sometimes agreed that letting male perpetrators off lightly tended to reflect a male dominated system. Comparisons were made with the severe sentences given to women who had committed violent acts against their male partner in response to ongoing violence.

(iv)   Possible consequences for the victim

It was felt that there could be significant consequences for the victim if the police and courts became involved. It was felt that it could provoke further violence from the partner, either immediately after the police had left or, if the man had been taken away, once he returned.

Financial consequences and hardships were also raised, with the possibility of any fines having to be paid from the household budget and the victim's own income.

> "Well if they get back together and the man gets fined, it's
> the wife that ends up paying, isn't it?"
> *(Female, 36 - 50 years, C2DE)*

There was also recognition of potential embarrassment if the police were involved and a trial ensued. Many respondents felt the victim would suffer from speculation by neighbours and the possibility of newspaper coverage of the case. Finally, there was concern expressed on the impact of these outcomes on other family members and, in particular, young children.

Thus for these reasons it was believed that police intervention may not always be the most appropriate course of action to take and that more discreet interventions may avoid some of these more damaging outcomes.

(v)   Overview

In conclusion, respondents generally took the view that domestic violence was <u>morally</u> wrong and therefore a crime in the moral sense. However, the majority of respondents were less clear about whether it was a crime in the <u>legal</u> sense, although there was general agreement that it <u>ought</u> to be. This confusion reflected perceptions that police activity was patchy, court activity minimal and convictions difficult to achieve. As with violence in general, the feeling that the legal system does not take domestic violence seriously, contributes to the perception that it is acceptable and therefore is not necessarily worthy of concern.

Importantly, these perceived inconsistencies and limited legal activity are likely to be hard to alter. Any attempt to emphasise the criminality of domestic violence is likely to be successful only if the courts and police themselves are seen to act in a manner consistent with this.

2.6   Summary

- There was widespread awareness of domestic violence but it was not at the forefront of respondents' perceptions of violence in general.

- Perceptions of domestic violence tended to be derived from general 'folk knowledge', direct and indirect experiences, and mass media.

- The issue of domestic violence evoked strong imagery. It was variously perceived as:

    - ongoing, escalating, hidden and malicious

- incorporating physical but also mental violence (beyond 'normal' fights)
- typically involving a male perpetrator and female victim
- potentially involving all social classes, although stereotypical working class images were deep-rooted
- potentially extensive but the prevalence was hard to determine as domestic violence is often hidden

- Various factors were seen as likely to contribute to domestic violence. These showed remarkable consistency with the experience of victims, indicating the validity of public perceptions.

  - initiation - alcohol, insecurity, upbringing and low income
  - continuation - practical and emotional dependency, age, loss of self esteem and self blame, and fear of potential consequences of leaving the relationship
  - turning points - children involved or extreme severe injury

There was little expectation of habitual abusers reforming, although it was felt that this might potentially happen among those in the early stages of developing such behaviour. While there was wide understanding of and sympathy for the victim's predicament, many respondents expressed incredulity at the victim's decision to remain within the relationship.

- Domestic violence was generally felt to be unacceptable. However, some circumstances in which it may not be so actively condemned emerged. For example, 'one-off' physical violence in the 'normal' conflict in a relationship and mutual, often drunken, public violence were both relatively less readily condemned. Much less acceptable was the 'grey' area of malicious ongoing male violence to a woman which was hidden and about which the public often had little direct experience and were uncertain how to act.

- Respondents' experiences of involvement as outsiders in situations of domestic violence was limited. Primarily this was conceptualised as helping the victim rather than the perpetrator. A mismatch was apparent between concern for the victim and uncertainty about whether, when and how to act, which would often mean protracted soul-searching. The main advice that would be offered to the victim would be offered was 'to get out' or 'to get help'. Any help and support given was visualised primarily after a violent episode, such as providing a 'listening ear'. At the time of abuse, calling in the police was relatively more likely than personal intervention.

- A range of support agencies were discussed, again for victims rather than perpetrators. Considerable concerns were raised about involving 'outsiders' and the possible consequences.

- There was a widespread belief that the activity of the police and judiciary in this area was minimal, although there was some isolated recognition of help and assistance being offered. It was, however, widely felt that more could and should be done.

- It was also felt that any attempt to emphasise the criminality of domestic violence would be undermined by perceived inactivity or ineffectiveness on the part of the courts and the police.

3.0 THE GENERAL PUBLIC'S RESPONSE TO THE CAMPAIGN

This section examines the response to the different elements of The Scottish Office campaign and comments on related campaigns running at the same time. The key elements comprise the forty second television commercial, (Section 3.1); the ten second television commercial (Section 3.2) together with the related telephone service and information pack (Section 3.3 and 3.4); and the 'Love and Hate' outdoor poster (Section 3.5). Finally, Section 3.6 provides a summary of the general public's response to the campaign as a whole.

3.1 Forty second television commercial

This section examines awareness of and response to the commercial in terms of recall, perceived target, perceived message and identification of source. (Stills illustrating the commercial are shown in Appendix 1.)

The commercial, because of its sensitive nature, was shown after the nine o'clock watershed. It was first shown on 16 June 1994 during the screening of the Football World Cup, in order to reach the male sections of the target audience. Screening continued until mid-July and was repeated in two week slots in October, November and December. The launch of the commercial received considerable prior attention from the media and the image of the bruised woman's face portrayed in the television commercial appeared in the national press (see Appendix Three). The research was designed in such a way that the first two focus group discussions were held prior to the first screening. The remaining eight were conducted at two stages after the launch.

Response to the commercial is explored in terms of awareness (Section 3.1.1), appeal (Section 3.1.2), interpretation (Section 3.1.3), perceived target and message (Sections 3.1.4 and 3.1.5) and identity and source (Section 3.1.6)

3.1.1 Awareness

The majority of respondents in the post-launch groups were aware of the commercial with many spontaneously recalling it when the topic of domestic violence was introduced to the discussions.

> "There's this horrific advert on the telly just now with them
> sitting in the pub and the female's face is getting worse and
> worse."
> *(Male, 36 - 50 years, ABC1)*

The remainder recognised the commercial when it was shown to them during the discussions. Awareness was higher for this than for any other element of the campaign.

Awareness was enhanced by the prior publicity with many respondents recalling having heard about the commercial from reading about it in the press and from seeing television features around the time of the launch (see Appendix Three). Some recalled actively looking out for the campaign as a result of this publicity.

> "They kept telling you about the advert coming up about
> violence. They showed you a slight clip."
> *(Female, 36 - 50 years, C2DE)*

> "I think everybody wanted to see it. They'd heard about it

and they wanted to see it."
(Female, 20 - 35 years, ABC1)

Many respondents described discussing the commercial with friends and colleagues before and after the early screenings. Parallels were drawn with drink-driving commercials, which had also generated considerable media interest and used hard-hitting imagery. Many recalled first seeing the commercial at the time of the World Cup. The fact that the timing of the launch was recalled even towards the end of the research (weeks and months afterwards) suggests that the commercial had an unusually high impact. The extensive publicity surrounding the launch is likely to be partly responsible for this.

"They (the TV commercials) were on after ten o'clock at night. Was it not when the World Cup was on?"
(Female, 20 - 35 years, C2DE)

It had clearly made a vivid impression on the majority of respondents and some were able to describe it in considerable detail. The most salient and vivid memory for many was of the progressive bruising on the face of the woman victim.

"That advert on the TV where the lassy gets worse and worse. I do feel very, very sorry for her. I feel very sad for her."
(Male, 36 - 50 years, C2DE)

3.1.2 Appeal

The commercial had considerable impact. It was seen as stronger and more graphic than those usually seen on television. The main impact was in the visual portrayal of the bruising developing on the woman's face. Thus, adjectives describing the commercial as a whole focussed on this aspect - *"gory"*, *"scary"*, *"horrific"*, *"it was a total shock to me"*. Some said they were reluctant to watch.

"I hate watching it. It sends shivers down me."
(Female, 20 - 35 years, C2DE)

This response seemed to reflect the commercial's perceived realism rather than to undermine its strengths. The majority of respondents felt that this level of horror was appropriate given the seriousness of the subject, and that the commercial showed, in a realistic and graphic way, something one would not normally see.

"It's true to life."
(Female, 20 - 35 years, ABC1)

"It's enough to make you stop and think ... anymore (would be) ridiculous."
(Female, 36 - 50 years, C2DE)

However, a small minority felt it was too violent.

"It makes me feel bad, sick. I just didn't like watching it."
(Female, 20 - 35 years, ABC1)

"It's not necessary to be that grotesque."
(Female, 20 - 35 years, ABC1)

> "That woman is really bad. I think her make-up is really
> good. It's a very well done advert, but I just don't like to
> see that at all."
> *(Female, 20 - 35 years, C2DE)*

In particular, there was concern that it was not suitable for children to watch. It was, however, agreed that children should at some point be made aware of the issue, perhaps in schools. It was also noted that children still watched television after the nine o'clock watershed and that it was therefore difficult to prevent them from seeing the commercial.

In contrast, a few individuals felt that the commercial was not hard hitting enough. These respondents compared it with the drink-driving commercials which showed *'dead bodies'* and felt that the campaign should go to those same extremes.

3.1.3 Interpretation

The storyline was intriguing to respondents. Most noticeably the respondents in the first two focus groups, who saw the commercial for the first time during the discussion group sessions asked to see it again in order to determine what was happening. Nearly all the respondents in the post-launch focus groups had seen it a number of times and had already come to their own conclusions about the storyline. Within these groups there were some variations in interpretation, although each individual felt confident in their understanding of the commercial.

The majority saw the commercial as clearly portraying domestic violence and showing the most obvious form, namely physical violence.

> "They are socialising and then gradually you see all the
> bruises."
> *(Female, 36 - 50 years, C2DE)*

Most felt that the man was recalling his violent behaviour and feeling remorse as a result.

> "She came in and as it goes on, her face is getting worse and
> worse as if he's thinking about it."
> *(Female, 36 - 50 years, C2DE)*

While there had been some initial confusion as to whether the abuse took place within the pub or that it was visible to all those sitting in the pub, most had come to the conclusion that this represented a flashback in the mind of the man as he remembered the damage he had inflicted on his partner. Thus, the bruises were understood to be a visual representation of the man's remorse.

An alternative interpretation, given by a few individuals, was that the appearance of the bruising and the man's expression reflected either his plans to beat the woman that night or the woman's anticipation of a beating.

> "It looks like he's going to hit her. He's thinking about
> doing it again."
> *(Female, 36 - 50 years, C2DE)*

A few others felt that he looked angry, perhaps because the woman had come to the pub and was showing her bruises.

> "He was angry, almost growling at her."
> *(Female, 20 - 35 years, ABC1)*

Another isolated interpretation was that he looked unconcerned, *"as if butter wouldn't melt in his mouth."*

The majority, however, felt that the man was remorseful; one or two said they had detected a tear in his eye.

Other minor variations in interpretation were concerned with whether or not the man and woman were married and whether or not they were still in a relationship. Most respondents felt that the relationship was over. Others debated who had arrived at the pub first and whether they were sitting together or at separate tables.

Despite these differences in interpretation, it was notable that most respondents felt they understood the storyline. In other words, the commercial did not appear to generate uncertainty or frustration because of any inability to decode its meaning. Many of the minor variations in interpretation are probably not important and even the more significant variations, concerning the timing of events and whether the man felt anger or remorse were not the only interpretation offered among those who mentioned them. As one woman reflected, when discussing the more detailed interpretations;

> "It doesn't matter how you are taking it, you are actually
> seeing it."
> *(Female, 20 - 35 years, ABC1)*

It was evident that these possible storylines had stimulated discussion with friends and colleagues when the commercial was first launched and had apparently seemed to increase interest and raise awareness, both of the commercial and of the issue of domestic violence.

Other background details of interest to the research included the perceived age and social class of the main characters. The two main characters were generally seen to be in their early thirties, which was considered appropriate in that it did not portray domestic violence as a young or old person's problem. In addition, the characters were not seen to fit the working class stereotype (see Section 2.2.3), in so far as they were not class specific.

> "I think the guy's trying to show that it's a normal thing as
> well ... It's not like a Rab C Nesbitt thing."
> *(Male, 20 - 35 years, ABC1)*

In addition, the choice of pub was seen as non class-specific. However, the pub location itself linked the theme of domestic violence with alcohol, which tended to confirm a perceived cause of this form of abuse.

Finally, the portrayal of physical violence together with a male perpetrator and female victim reflected the main image most respondents held of domestic violence. However, it was not seen to portray mental or sexual abuse and so did not reflect the range of violence most respondents felt was experienced by victims. In addition, focussing on facial bruising tended not to reflect the view generally held by respondents that victims were usually beaten on parts of the body that would be concealed by clothes.

3.1.4 Perceived target

Most respondents felt that those immediately involved in domestic violence were the intended target group for the commercial but unsure whether the key group was male perpetrators or female victims.

On first viewing the commercial, male perpetrators of violence tended to be seen as the prime target group. This perception was also apparent immediately after the commercial was viewed during the discussion sessions. This view was reinforced by the perception that the commercial had been launched to coincide with peak male television viewing for the Football World Cup.

> "I think the TV one was mainly for men, especially being on during the World Cup."
> *(Female, 20 - 35 years, C2DE)*

However, those respondents interviewed nearer the end of the fieldwork, when they were discussing the commercial from memory, tended to feel that the commercial was targeted primarily at female victims. This is perhaps because the image of the bruised face of the woman was the most memorable image in the commercial.

The general public was not generally seen as a target.

> "I think it's specifically aimed at the people who are involved in it, because the whole thing is to decide if you've done that you're guilty, but if you haven't done that, or you're not involved in that, well you don't have to worry."
> *(Male, 20 - 35 years, ABC1)*

The respondents did not spontaneously see themselves as the target and did not agree when this possibility was suggested by the moderator. As one respondent said:

> "If it was society, it would say, 'When will <u>we</u> face up to it?'"
> *(Male, 20 - 35 years, ABC1)*

> "I think it would need to be happening to you before you'd notice."
> *(Female, 36 - 50 years, C2DE)*

However, during the discussion it was apparent that the commercial was reaching this general public sample, in that it clearly contributed to raising awareness of the issue and a feeling of outrage that such acts of violence took place.

3.1.5 Perceived message

As the commercial was seen to target both male perpetrators and female victims, it was seen to contain two main messages.

Firstly, it was seen to be trying to encourage male perpetrators to change their violent behaviour.

> "The message I got was really the guy realising he's got to stop ... really showing him what damage he had done ... the next stage is for that guy to say 'I'm doing something I shouldn't. I need help.'"
> *(Male, 36 - 50 years, ABC1)*

This was seen as a valid and worthwhile message.

> "If it only stops one wife beater. It if only makes one of them stop and think, it's worth it."
> *(Female, 36 - 50 years, C2DE)*

The mass media approach was considered particularly relevant since most respondents felt that perpetrators were likely to keep their actions hidden and to avoid facing up to the harm they caused. The commercial was seen as a stimulus or catalyst to provoke perpetrators to examine their behaviour.

> "If they have blinkers on when they are doing it and then they are actually seeing somebody else in front of them and then they are thinking, 'Oh God, I actually do that.'"
> *(Female, 20 - 35 years, C2DE)*

> "There could be guys who hit their wives and they don't like what they do. Maybe they would phone. Even if it was one, one less woman getting beaten up, it would be a help"
> *(Female, 20 - 35 years, C2DE)*

However, many respondents were not convinced that this message would reach perpetrators.

> "That's not going to stop someone who's beating their wife. If they're angry or they're drunk or they've lost control."
> *(Male, 36 - 50 years, ABC1)*

> "We (the public) do take them on board but whether it's actually aimed to prevent or stop, whether they (perpetrators) take it on board or whether they just turn their face up to it, I don't know ..."
> *(Male, 36 - 50 years, ABC1)*

It was, however, hoped that the commercial would at least make perpetrators think about their actions. It was considered that this was more likely to happen with perpetrators in the early stages of abuse than with habitual abusers.

> "Maybe if a man was going to do that and he was sitting watching that, he would think about it ... but there are them who hit their partners everyday and it wouldn't make a blind bit of difference to the likes of them."
> *(Female, 36 - 50 years, C2DE)*

> "I think someone who's maybe just hit their wife once or twice, they would maybe take more notice."
> *(Female, 36 - 50 years, C2DE)*

For female victims, the message was generally seen to be one of recognition, that society is aware that this form of violence occurs. Some respondents felt the commercial was encouraging victims to face up to the situation and *"get out"*.

> "If this act is there, it has been hidden from their friends. They're out socialising, she's not got a mark on her, but she's still with him and it's a case of 'When will you (the woman) face up to it?'"
> *(Male, 36 - 50 years, ABC1)*

> "If the women are watching it that are being abused then it is a contact for help."
> *(Female, 20 - 35 years, C2DE)*

As far as the general public was concerned, most respondents felt that these messages were only salient to those who were in close contact with someone in the situation portrayed in the commercial.

> "Well it's not relevant to me. I don't know anybody at the
> moment. If I knew a neighbour ..."
> *(Female, 20 - 35 years, C2DE)*

However, it was clear the commercial raised awareness of the issue and aroused feelings of condemnation.

> "I think it really brings home the message that we don't see
> that."
> *(Female, 20 - 35 years, C2DE)*

> "Not walk away the next time when they see it happen."
> *(Female, 20 - 35 years, C2DE)*

In addition it conveyed new information, namely that domestic violence is a crime in the moral as well as the legal sense, and that the police could therefore be informed of violent situations. However, there was still some scepticism about the likelihood of effective policing or of the courts taking a more serious attitude towards domestic violence (see Section 2.5.3).

Perpetrators themselves supported this view, arguing that the fact that domestic violence is a criminal offence did not act as a deterrent. In addition, the criminality message was seen as secondary to the strong emotional and moral message conveyed in the storyline.

> "The shock of seeing that woman battered is more than it
> being a criminal offence."
> *(Male, 36 - 50 years, ABC1)*

Finally, most respondents did not recognise any suggestions about how to act in relation to situations of domestic violence, either as a participant or an observer. The ten second television commercial which did invite action by telephoning for help and advice was not widely recalled (see Section 3.2.1).

> "There's nothing in that to say where to go is there? For
> either person to go? If this is happening to you as a female
> or are you the person who is doing this? Call or whatever.
> I'm wondering if someone did say, 'Oh Christ, I do beat my
> wife.' (what would they do?)."
> *(Male, 36 - 50 years, ABC1)*

This lack of awareness often led to the criticism that the campaign failed to provide the necessary follow-up and support for those most in need of it.

3.1.6 Identity and source

The commercial was generally referred to as either *"the one with the battered woman in the pub"* or just *"the TV commercial about domestic violence."* It was not normally referred to by the slogan 'It's a crime', although a few respondents referred to this element of the campaign when discussing the legality of domestic violence. Similarly, it was not referred to as having been commissioned by The Scottish Office, although a few respondents were able to name The Scottish Office as the source when asked. When informed that The Scottish Office was the source, many respondents appeared vague about its function, although most connected it with 'the Government'.

The commercial was often linked with other publicity, such as the 'Love and Hate' poster, the ten second television commercial and Zero Tolerance material[1], all of which focussed on the domestic violence issue. Indeed, some respondents thought the commercial might have been produced by Zero Tolerance. This was primarily in the East of Scotland where awareness of elements of the Zero Tolerance campaign was much higher, reflecting longer periods of exposure to the campaign.

The forty second television commercial and the other campaign material were seen as part of a wider groundswell of media interest in the subject of domestic violence, although respondents were not clear from where each element actually came. However, the source of these domestic violence campaigns was not an area of concern for them with the exception of the telephone service (see Section 3.3.2). Victims commented that they were pleased that The Scottish Office recognised their situation, but some were also resentful that resources spent on the campaign were not paralleled by resources spent on support agencies (see Section 5.2.3).

3.1.7 Overview

The commercial showed considerable strengths but also some potential weaknesses. These are listed below:

- It was clearly seen to be about domestic violence and reflected an issue which was considered important. It was felt to demonstrate also that The Scottish Office was taking a responsible attitude to a serious issue. It was seen as part of a broader media movement to raise awareness of domestic violence and to open up a previously hidden and taboo issue.

- It had a high impact and left a strong moral and emotional impression. It promoted discussion of the issue, at least at the time of the launch.

- It evoked abhorrence and outrage in relation to domestic violence among the general public.

- It delivered the message that domestic violence is wrong and that perpetrators should face up to their actions. The statement that 'domestic violence is a crime' was believed and provided new information for those less well informed.

- It was seen as being aimed at two target groups, primarily male perpetrators but also female victims. It was seen to speak directly to perpetrators, encouraging them to examine and to change their behaviour. It was also seen as indirectly telling female victims that their problem was recognised and encouraging them to seek help. This theme was more enduring because of the impact of the woman's bruised face.

- There were different interpretations of the storyline which could potentially dilute its impact. Some respondents thought that the man was planning a future beating and was therefore expressing anger rather than remorse.

- To an extent, the commercial reinforced some of the stereotypical images of domestic violence. There was a focus on physical rather than mental violence and a link with alcohol was implied, which, together with the launch during the Football World Cup, could reinforce an association with working class men.

---

[1] The Zero Tolerance campaign was first launched by Edinburgh District Council Women's Committee in December 1992. The campaign publicised a range of aspect of violence against women, addressing domestic violence, child sexual abuse, rape and sexual assault. The media used comprise posters and placards, leaflets, bookmarks and badges, incorporating the 'Z' logo. The campaign has been adopted by other local authorities. It was launched by Strathclyde Regional Council in March 1994 in partnership with District Councils, Health Boards, women's organisations and other agencies.

- The portrayal of domestic violence by focusing on visible facial bruising was not felt to reflect the public's existing awareness of the wide range of physical and mental abuse women experience. In addition, there was awareness that if a woman was struck, it was unlikely to be on the face but instead would be on parts of the body where it could not be readily seen by outsiders. Victims groups were also concerned about these aspects.

- There was a perception that the commercial would be unlikely to stimulate a change in behaviour among perpetrators and in particular among habitual abusers. Only those at the early stages of developing such behaviour were seen as likely to react to advertising.

- It was felt that although attention was drawn to the victims' plight, no clear offer of help and support was made. The ten second television commercial which attempted to do this was rarely recalled and was not clearly linked to the forty second television commercial (see below).

- The 'domestic violence is a crime' message tended not to be well remembered at an unprompted level. It was also felt that the criminal status of domestic violence was unlikely to be a deterrent to offenders, and many were sceptical about how seriously the police and courts would treat a domestic violence incident.

- Finally and importantly, the commercial is not seen as speaking directly to the general public. The main targets and messages revolve around perpetrators and victims. The commercial confirms the seriousness of the problem and raises awareness of the issue but does not challenge the public to make any personal contribution or give any guidance about what that contribution might be. This was contrasted with the Zero Tolerance materials which challenged public attitudes. However, there is scope for enlisting more active support of the public by, for example, giving guidance on how to help, demonstrating police willingness to act, and by emphasising how flippant comments can both reflect and lead to tolerance of domestic violence.

3.2 Ten second television commercial

The ten second television commercial comprised three frames with individual straplines on a black background (see Appendix 1). In the background the voices of a man and a woman are heard, the man saying he is sorry and the woman sobbing. The final frame gives a freephone number, inviting calls from victims, offenders or concerned others.

3.2.1 Awareness

Respondents were much less aware of this commercial than of the forty second television commercial. They rarely mentioned it spontaneously in the context of domestic violence and tended only to recall it when talking about the need for support services in connection with the main commercial. However, a few did link it with the main commercial, and others recalled the existence of a telephone line but were unsure where they had seen it promoted.

On further prompting, those who could recall the commercial had difficulty in remembering details. Often the memory was of a black screen with text. Some could remember that the text included a phoneline number and a list of potential users, and only a few were able to recall these as victims, perpetrators and connected others.

3.2.2 Perceived target

The target was seen to be those groups listed in the final frame of the commercial, namely victims, perpetrators and connected others. These groups were felt to be in legitimate need of information or support. In this respect the commercial was perceived to fulfil the need for support already identified and found lacking in the main commercial but, as already stated, it was not strongly linked to the main commercial.

Victims were seen as the main target and believed to be most likely to make use of a telephone service. It was felt that perpetrators would be less likely to admit the existence of a problem. Finally, it was presumed that connected others such as relatives, friends and neighbours, might be reluctant to get involved.

3.2.3 Perceived message

The message was clearly communicated as a support theme, for example, it was not misinterpreted as a 'report line.' As discussed below (see Section 3.3) it was assumed that the commercial was promoting a telephone advice and counselling service designed to give support, primarily to victims of domestic violence.

3.2.4 Identity and source

As with the main commercial, this was seen as part of a range of media approaches addressing the issue of domestic violence (see Section 3.1.6). The source of the commercial was not questioned except in relation to the telephone service itself (see Section 3.3.2).

3.2.5 Overview

The main strength of the commercial was that, since it was perceived to offer support which would meet the needs aroused by the forty second television commercial, it could potentially add credibility to the campaign as a whole.

However, some criticisms emerged:

- Many failed to recall the commercial whilst those that did, did not always link it to the main commercial. As a result its potential to enhance and support the forty second television commercial was limited.

- There were also perceived to be some inconsistencies between the tone and message of the forty second television commercial which focused on legality and the ten second television commercial which offered support and help. It was argued that this would discourage perpetrators from using the service for fear of legal action. However, this was not of concern to the general public given their preference for retribution rather than rehabilitation.

- It was felt that the ten second televison commercial did not give sufficient encouragement to telephone. For example, assurances of confidentiality were considered important for both victims and perpetrators and were not given.

3.3 The telephone service

The freephone telephone service was promoted by the ten second television commercial. Callers receive a recorded message with a female voice which thanks them for calling and suggests that if they need emergency help they contact the Police, Women's Aid or Social Work Departments for which the local numbers can be found in the telephone directory. Callers are also invited to leave a name and address (perhaps not their own) to which an information pack can be sent.

This section explores response to the concept of a telephone service, together with response to the current initiative.

3.3.1 Response to the concept

The concept of a telephone service was enthusiastically received. It was appreciated and seen as essential that a freephone number be offered.

Basing their opinions on the promotion of the service by the ten second television commercial, most respondents in all the focus groups anticipated that it would act as a crisis or helpline service similar in style to that offered by the Samaritans or Childline. It was widely expected that it would be staffed on a 24 hour basis and that there would be trained counsellors available who would be able to listen objectively to the situation and offer confidential advice and follow-up if requested. More specifically it was anticipated that they would be able to suggest local contacts and give back up as required.

> "... a calm female telling you what to do and numbers to phone ..."
> "... a Samaritan person ..."
> "... a person for contacts and advice."
> *(Females, 20 - 35 years, C2DE)*

> "I thought it would be a Samaritan-type thing, Childline, something like that."
> *(Female, 20 - 35 years, C2DE)*

> "Somebody like the Samaritans or Women's Aid or Men's Aid or whatever you want to call it. It's someone who'll give you advice or can offer help from the social services."
> *(Male, 36 - 50 years, ABC1)*

It was felt that female victims would tend to welcome outside objective advice. Many, although not all, of the general public sample said that they would go to outsiders rather than family or friends if they had a domestic problem (see Section 2.5). It was felt in situations of domestic violence that a stranger would have a calmer outlook and be unbiased, whereas a relative might say, *"I told you so"*, apportion blame or even defend the perpetrator.

Importantly, it was also believed that contacting a confidential telephone counselling service would not result in unwanted outside interference. In this sense, the telephone service was seen to offer an attractive alternative to contacting the police or social services, which could result in pressure to press charges or moves to take children into care (see Section 2.5).

> "Saying you are not actually involved, the number is there, which is quite good."
> *(Female, 20 - 35 years, C2DE)*

The main user group was seen to be female victims rather than male perpetrators. Many respondents felt that males would be unwilling to admit they had a problem or to seek help with the possible exception of those who had not yet established patterns of habitual abuse.

Most respondents, therefore, thought that the primary need was friendly, objective support and practical advice on the options open to victims and how to anticipate and overcome obstacles.

> "An offender isn't going to phone it."
> *(Male, 36 - 50 years, ABC1)*

> "Stand up and confront it and most people just need that little shove and that bit of support and if you've got somebody on the phone saying, 'Look, you really have to end this, do something.'"
> *(Male, 36 - 50 years, ABC1)*

None of the respondents who took part in the research said that they had contemplated using the phoneline.

Most respondents said that they assumed that the female victim would have to pluck up considerable courage to use the telephone service and would often be in an extremely emotional state. A scenario frequently envisaged by both male and female respondents was of the woman running away from a violent situation, perhaps with her children, wearing only her nightclothes, with no money and calling from a public call box.

The highly emotional nature of the perceived contact with the telephone service further highlighted the need for, and expectation of, a full counselling service.

3.3.2 Response to the service

There was widespread shock and resentment on learning through the research that the service was limited to a dissemination exercise. This response was expressed consistently in all the general public groups, both male and female.

> "Oh my goodness, that's awful. I think that's dreadful that."
> *(Female, 20 - 35 years, C2DE)*

It was strongly argued that callers would feel badly let down by receiving a recorded message.

> "If you are crying your eyes out and you think, 'I must do something' and you've gathered up all your strength and it's your first wee thing of confidence to pick up that telephone."
> *(Female, 20 - 35 years, C2DE)*

> "I think people that phone these things, finding the courage to chat , the number, you want instant help."
> *(Female, 20 - 35 years, ABC1)*

> "If I was a woman who was getting beat up and I saw that I'd have thought 'a lifeline' and phoned it and got a tape. I'd be at the end of my tether. She's wanting a shoulder to cry on, someone to speak to, not a tape recorder."
> *(Male, 36 - 50 years, ABC1)*

The recorded message was criticised for being unhelpful and impractical as well as inappropriate. For example, it was argued that there might not be a telephone directory available to look up other numbers, the woman might not have any money with her to make further calls or have a paper and pencil to write down other numbers.

> "She could be 'phoning from a public call box - no pencil,
> no money, she's desperate."
> *(Female, 36 - 50 years, C2DE)*

Most respondents also reacted negatively to the concept of answerphones in general. Many felt anxious or unwilling to leave a message, even in more mundane circumstances. The usual reaction was to put the telephone down again on hearing a recorded message.

> "You put it down right away."
> *(Female, 36 - 50 years, C2DE)*

It was therefore considered even more daunting to use an answerphone in the difficult and emotional circumstances connected with domestic violence.

> "If you really sincerely wanted to help people then you
> would have a manned phoneline."
> *(Female, 20 - 35 years, C2DE)*

Problems of confidentiality were also highlighted. It was widely recognised that it would be difficult to have a pack sent to the victim's own house, because of the potential reaction of partners.

> "Especially if you got a pack through the post and the person
> who beats you picks it up and says, 'What the hell is this?'
> You'd get another beating, wouldn't you!"
> *(Male, 36 - 50 years, ABC1)*

Giving an alternative address, as suggested in the message, was also seen as difficult by many if a woman had not told anyone about her situation and did not want to do so. This was confirmed by victims themselves. They agreed that materials could not have been sent to their own house but felt it would also have been difficult to use someone else's address. Many had had their freedom restricted and were not 'allowed' by their partner to spend time with friends outside the home (see Section 5.1.3).

Evidently the public had expectations that the service would be addressing the problem in a more proactive manner than was the case. Interestingly, it was at this point in the discussion that respondents expressed an interest in the source of the material. Their cynicism was enhanced when they learnt that it was sponsored by The Scottish Office or 'the Government'.

> "I think that's typical of the Government. Actually it's pretty
> poor."
> *(Male, 36 - 50 years, ABC1)*

> "Typical, eh?"
> *(Female, 20 - 35 years, C2DE)*

Many felt that it was money wasted and contrasted the cost of the advertisements to the cost of providing a telephone counselling service which was perceived as essential.

> "Somebody should write in about that. That is totally
> dreadful. All the money the government wastes. What
> happens if that lady is standing on the street and she has two

weans or something."
(Female, 36 - 50 years, C2DE)

"It's a waste of money. What's the point? It's costing millions to put the adverts out."
(Female, 36 - 50 years, C2DE)

"If they're serious about a campaign you can't go half-hearted into something ... they spent quite a lot on the adverts getting them very professional and very well done and at the end - 'Bugger it, we've run out of money, we'll just put a tape recorder at the end.'"
(Male, 36 - 50 years, ABC1)

"I'm really shocked about that, deary me. I know there's a lot of money goes into this."
(Female, 20 - 35 years, C2DE)

"They've gone to the bother of a fantastic advert, it's so effective and they follow up by having a tape recorded message."
(Male, 36 - 50 years, ABC1)

3.3.3 Overview

The provision of a freephone telephone service was considered an essential element of the campaign. It was expected to provide confidential, objective, personal counselling along with practical advice and contact with relevant support services. Respondents were shocked to learn that the service provided was a recorded message and leaflet request service when the potential users were typically assumed to be in extreme emotional distress. It was therefore anticipated that callers would be considerably let down by such as service. It was also considered unlikely that they would feel able to leave a message or to make the follow-on calls suggested by the recorded message because of fear of reprisals and practical difficulties.

3.4 The information pack

The information pack is sent to callers to the freephone telephone service who leave their name and address. It is sent in a brown A5 size envelope and comprises leaflets giving contact numbers for Women's Aid and Victim Support, a leaflet designed for perpetrators and a police leaflet about general safety for women, called 'Talking Sense.' It was not within the scope of research to explore response to the material in detail, but respondents were given the opportunity to examine the contents. The following responses emerged in relation to the concept and the materials.

3.4.1 Response to the concept

Respondents tended to dismiss the concept of a leaflet pack. It was generally felt that personal contact was more important.

"I don't think that at a time like that a leaflet is worth a damn. You're far better with a human being."

For both victims and perpetrators, most respondents felt that personal contact was more useful since a listening ear and objective support were seen to be as or more important than basic information. Where practical information was required, they felt that it needed to be tailored to individual needs and local service provision. This pointed towards the need for personal contacts at a local level. It was also felt that direct referral to relevant agencies was more effective than the victim having to undertake further attempts to make contact themselves.

In addition, as discussed above, it was believed that victims would find it difficult to send for such materials (see Section 3.3.2).

However, in different circumstances, literature was felt to have an important role to play in promoting and disseminating information about domestic violence and available services. For example, isolated suggestions were blanket distribution of written information either house-to-house as in the initial leafleting about HIV/AIDS in the 1980s or through child benefit books. This, it was believed, could minimise any repercussions from perpetrators finding literature in the house since the victim would not have sent for it. Other suggestions included the use of literature to reinforce advice given face-to-face.

3.4.2 Response to the materials

Overall, the diverse and fragmented nature of the material, both in terms of design and content, conveyed an impression that the exercise had been poorly co-ordinated and had not sought to address the needs of those most likely to make use of the service. For example, the leaflets were visually diverse using a variety of formats and layouts. In addition, items such as the 'Talking Sense' booklet and references to marriage guidance counselling services were considered extraneous and inappropriate materials for those immediately concerned about violent domestic situations.

The leaflets respondents tended to consider most relevant were those giving local contact numbers for organisations such as Women's Aid and Victim Support. However, many respondents were disappointed to learn of the restricted hours shown for many of the telephone services. It was believed that 'around the clock' services were required.

The perpetrators' leaflet was recognised as being designed specifically for the campaign. At first glance, it was seen as more accessible in that it was short, to the point, and contained useful headings. However, the content tended not to be seen as giving realistic advice which, in part, reflected the perception that abusers were unlikely to change. In particular, many respondents commented on the advice to the perpetrator about 'walking away' when a potentially violent situation was developing. Such logical advice was felt to be irrelevant, unrealistic and misunderstood the irrational nature of domestic violence. This perception was confirmed by respondents from victims' groups. For example, one victim's husband had actually discussed such a strategy with her but, in her experience, it had been ineffective in the heat of the moment.

3.4.3 Overview

Respondents were generally dismissive of the value of the pack, both at a conceptual, and executional level. It was felt that receiving and reading such material undetected would be problematic. It was also felt that the contents of the pack itself were diverse and fragmented, suggesting poor co-ordination and a failure to recognise and address the needs of key caller groups.

3.5 'Love and Hate' outdoor poster

This poster depicted two clenched fists with the knuckles foremost. Each knuckle was tattooed to spell out the words Love and Hate (Appendix 1). It was primarily displayed on billboards but also designed for use in A3 format for public noticeboards. This section describes respondents' awareness of the materials, and their perceptions of the target and message, together with perceptions of identity and source.

3.5.1 Awareness

There was relatively high awareness of the poster but only in the billboard format. It was more likely to be mentioned spontaneously than the ten second television commercial in the context of discussion about domestic violence, but much less likely to be mentioned in this way than the main forty second television commercial. Many others recognised it when prompted. Awareness was higher among males and in the East. It is probable that overall awareness was high for an outdoor poster of this type, although no normative data exists. The poster was described vividly by those who had seen it.

"I nearly, in fact almost, hit the car in front (when I saw it)."
(Male, Mixed Group, 36 - 50 years, ABC1)

It was seen by most respondents as portraying the hands of a strong male. The man was perceived as most likely to be working class and physically tough. The size of the fist and the hairs on the fingers reinforced these perceptions. Words like *"navvy"*, *"biker"* and *"labourers"* were frequently used when describing the character and there was widespread agreement that the clenched fists conveyed an image of violence. Thus, the advertisement confirmed the stereotype image of the perpetrator of domestic violence as being 'rough' and working class. In addition, some commented on sightings opposite pubs which supported the perceived connection between alcohol and domestic violence. The ring worn on the left hand was frequently commented on as suggesting violence within a marriage.

"I'll tell you what struck me straight away, when I saw the
one that's got the hate on, it has a wedding ring on it."
(Male, 36 - 50 years, ABC1)

Thus the poster had considerable impact, contained powerful and provocative imagery and was easily linked with the subject area, reflecting as it did the stereotyped perceptions of a typical perpetrator.

3.5.2 Perceived target and message

Perceptions of the specific target and message of the poster were unclear, although the imagery itself was clearly connected with the topic area.

It was argued by most respondents that logically the poster should be aimed at perpetrators of domestic violence.

"It's obviously aimed at the instigator of the violence."
(Male, Mixed Group, 36 - 50 years, ABC1)

However, the poster was not generally seen to confront perpetrators in the same way as the television commercials. Some argued that it could potentially offer support to perpetrators in their defiance of 'the system' by conveying empowering images of violence and hatred.

Indeed, one of the perpetrators interviewed actually wore these symbols with pride. Some female respondents thought men might make light of it among their friends and envisaged groups of men leaving the pub near a billboard poster, asking each other, *"which one will you give her tonight?"*.

Finally, the poster was seen as unlikely to engage the general public although the memorable and striking image did have an awareness raising effect.

> "That affects certain people. I don't really read the posters because it's never happened that and it doesn't really affect me. I don't know anyone who beats their wives up. I don't see any wives going around with black eyes so ..."
> *(Male, 36 - 50 years, ABC1)*

Some female respondents however found it threatening.

> "It's horrible."
> *(Female, 20 - 35 years, ABC1)*

> "It's what she sees, coming down at her."
> *(Female, 20 - 35 years, ABC1)*

Similarly the poster was not found to have relevance to victims except in negative terms. Some found it threatening and said it brought back memories of their own experiences.

The message conveyed was also ambiguous. Interpretations ranged from a message that there was both a 'warm' and a 'dark side' to a relationship, to the totally uncompromising message that hate equals violence and love equals rape.

> "To make them feel bad that's doing it."
> *(Female, Mixed Group, 36 - 50 years, ABC1)*

> "I thought it didn't matter which one he gave her, it would still hurt."
> *(Male, 36 - 50 years, ABC1)*

There was concern expressed about the effectiveness of the poster, or indeed any poster, in terms of modifying behaviour.

> "Whether that would change somebody from beating his wife. I don't think that seeing a poster would stop any of these people that are that way inclined doing that."
> *(Male, 36 - 50 years, ABC1)*

> "All the ten or twenty percent that do it (violence) they're not all going to jump up and say, 'Oh, that advert is right, I've been a bad bugger all my life.' It might only affect one percent. I suppose if it does even one percent it's been a success."
> *(Male, 36 - 50 years, ABC1)*

Notable in these comments is an underlying assumption that the poster is speaking to perpetrators and not to the general public.

3.5.3 Identity and source

The poster was not readily linked with the television commercials since the imagery was seen to be distinct. However, like the television commercials, it was seen as part of the current and varied media coverage of the domestic violence issue. Any links that were made tended to be with Zero Tolerance materials, possibly because of the poster medium and the challenging nature of the imagery. This connection was more often made in the East than in the West of Scotland.

3.5.4 Overview

The 'Love and Hate' poster generated considerable awareness. It had high impact and conveyed powerful provocative images in an easily absorbed manner.

However, the message was ambiguous and some felt it could be counter-productive in that it could support male perpetrators in their behaviour or be threatening to women in general, particularly those who were victims of domestic violence.

A further drawback was that it reinforced the commonly held stereotype that perpetrators of such violence were typically working class, 'rough', 'criminal' types.

In addition, it was not clearly linked with the remainder of The Scottish Office campaign, although it was seen as part of the varied media coverage of the domestic violence issue at the time.

3.6 Summary of the general public's response to the campaign

This summarises the general public's response to the campaign as a whole. Six areas are explored, namely, the campaign's impact, appeal, communication, credibility, salience and congruence with other materials. These highlight the main strengths and weaknesses of the campaign.

3.6.1 Impact

There were high levels of recall and recognition for the campaign elements, the forty second television commercial being most prominent. This impact was especially significant in the West where media activity relating to domestic violence was limited. In comparison, in the Edinburgh area, long term exposure to the Zero Tolerance campaign had already stimulated considerable awareness of the issue.

3.6.2 Appeal

The campaign was seen to have considerable appeal, with the forty second television commercial generating the most positive response. The campaign was seen to be well produced and executed and delivered a clear message. It was graphically distinct and stood out from the commercial advertising that predominates in the campaign's chosen media.

3.6.3 Communication

The campaign communicates at two levels, affective and cognitive.

At the affective level it aroused strong emotions, evoking abhorrence and condemnation of domestic violence. This is consistent with the campaign's stated aims. However, the research methodology was not designed to assess whether this abhorrence translates into long term changes in acceptability.

At the cognitive level it provided new information for some individuals, most notably that domestic violence is a crime in legal as well as moral terms. However, it should be noted that some disputed the credibility of these messages, arguing that the actions of the courts and the police suggest that the authorities do not necessarily take these offences seriously. In addition many did not define 'one hit' as domestic violence, categorising it instead as ongoing and malicious.

There were also some communication weaknesses. First, it was not seen as a discrete campaign. Of the three key elements, the two television commercials were broadly complementary, although few spontaneously linked them together, while the third element, the 'Love and Hate' outdoor poster, was seen to be quite distinct and separate. Secondly, the campaign was not seen to have a central identity, unlike the Zero Tolerance campaign, for example, which has achieved a generic label. Thirdly, there were some executional problems with the forty second television commercial although these tended not to interfere with the main message. Indeed, arguably these were responsible for creating debate.

Finally, the material had a tendency to promote a stereotypical picture of domestic violence. For example, domestic violence was shown in physical terms, with a male perpetrator and female victim; alcohol was inadvertently identified as a contributory cause through the choice of setting for the forty second television commercial; and, perhaps most significant of all, the 'Love and Hate' outdoor poster portrayed perpetrators as 'rough,' 'working class' 'criminal' types. It should, however, be noted that some of these portrayals are perhaps unavoidable. For example, promoting the criminality of the offence dictates the need to focus upon physical as opposed to mental forms of violence and abuse.

3.6.4 Credibility

Importantly, the campaign commanded considerable respect and credibility because it focused on an issue which many felt needed to be addressed and was seen to be trying to bring perpetrators to justice. Respondents made comparisons with campaigns addressing similar taboo subjects, such as child abuse, and complimented the campaign for giving prominence to the domestic violence issue in much the same way.

However, this credibility had only face validity because the support elements - the telephone service and information pack - were seen to be particularly weak in failing to provide access to what was considered appropriate advice and counselling support. The public, however, remain largely unaware of these perceived weaknesses.

3.6.5 Salience

Salience represents one of the campaign's weaknesses. Although the campaign is distinctive, creative and powerful, it does not communicate a message that the public at large can take away and build on. In other words, it does not challenge their views with regard to the subject area.

For example, although raising awareness of the problem and providing new information for some, it does not then go on to address the public's role, if any, in helping to resolve the situation, for example, addressing the contradictory attitudes towards this area of violence and how these condone domestic violence or highlighting the actions people might usefully take when confronted with an act of domestic violence and how these actions may vary depending upon the circumstances.

Instead, the real salience of the campaign is seen to lie with the perpetrators and victims. This has the effect of reinforcing the belief that the public do not have an active role to play in dealing with this form of violence.

3.6.6 Congruence

The research sought to explore whether the campaign was consistent with other messages appearing in the media at the same time. Overall, there were no obvious inconsistencies. The campaign tended to contribute to, rather than contradict other domestic violence themes and messages of which the public were aware.

The only problem to emerge lay with the 'Love and Hate' outdoor poster which was seen to brand perpetrators of this type of violence as working class. This was identified as inconsistent with the Zero Tolerance campaign which, it was claimed, attempts to highlight the fact that domestic violence is a reality in all walks of life and in all social groups.

3.6.7 Overview

Overall, the campaign was broadly consistent with the aims set regarding the general public. Thus, it aroused the appropriate emotions of abhorrence and condemnation and also provided new information for those less informed.

However, some potential weaknesses were apparent. Significantly, the support services did not match expectations and were not seen to meet the needs they were likely to arouse. The campaign was also seen to be aimed primarily at perpetrators and victims rather than the public themselves and hence did not challenge the public's own attitudes, nor give guidance on how to behave with regard to domestic violence. Finally, some elements of the campaign, most notably the outdoor poster, conveyed inappropriate and inconsistent images.

4.0 THE PERPETRATORS' PERSPECTIVE

This section examines response to the campaign from the perpetrators' perspective. As described in Section One, one group of male perpetrators was interviewed. These respondents were currently taking part in a programme for violent men and agreed to participate when approached by programme leaders. The findings here form both a retrospective and reflective view of the campaign in the light of their experience as a perpetrator. Thus perpetrators responded in terms of how they actually reacted and how they might have reacted to the campaign at the time of exposure to it.

The campaign was intended to work at two levels: first, to create a climate of abhorrence which would indirectly influence perpetrators (Section 4.1) and secondly, to directly encourage the male perpetrator to think about his actions (Section 4.2). These effects are explored in terms of both the punitive and supportive aspects of the campaign.

4.1 Indirect effects

The intended indirect effect of the campaign, as previously discussed, was to stimulate and enhance existing public outrage and abhorrence of the crime and in so doing create a social climate where domestic violence is considered unacceptable.

The perpetrators were aware, like the public, that the issue was being given prominence, with campaigns such as Zero Tolerance contributing to what was seen as a climate of intolerance. However, perpetrators had not, to their knowledge, experienced any personal interventions or approaches of any nature, aggressive or otherwise, that had been prompted by the campaign or the associated publicity.

Any indirect effects that could take place were seen to be more likely to occur through immediate family and friends who would be aware of their behaviour rather than via the public at large who would be unfamiliar with their personal circumstances and more reluctant to become involved. In this way personal friends and family rather than the public at large were considered the main agents of change and therefore a key target to facilitate any change that campaigns might bring about in the future.

In the final analysis, it is not possible for this research to assess whether eliciting public abhorrence and outrage has had any impact, helpful or otherwise, on perpetrators' behaviour. This would require a longitudinal experimental design. It is however, fair to surmise that any effect that has taken place over the duration of the campaign is likely to be subtle and its relationship with the specific campaign complex and difficult to assess, given the multitude of mediating factors.

4.2 Direct effects

The campaign encompassed both a punitive and supportive approach. The punitive approach was evident in the forty second television commercial. It implied a demand for retribution for crimes committed by highlighting the criminal aspect of the offence and by focussing upon the issue of guilt and shame. The supportive approach is reflected in the ten second television commercial and the provision of the telephone information service which directs callers towards sources of advice and help.

All perpetrators recognised that the campaign related to them since it tackled an issue that was relevant and specific to their experience and circumstances. It was more relevant to them than the Zero Tolerance campaign which was seen to cover a broader range of abuse.

How perpetrators then proceeded to consume or use the advertising, was dependent upon the degree to which they accepted responsibility for their behaviour. Two patterns of behaviour were evident in the discussions, namely denial and readiness to confront their actions. However, it should be remembered that the prevalence of these two behaviours within the perpetrator community is unknown and that there may be other patterns of response not picked up by the research.

4.2.1 Denial

Those who were at a stage of denial acknowledged no or little responsibility for their actions.

> "You come back to the house, even sitting in the house it can
> happen. It's not you, you're just maybe watching the telly,
> then you just change, your mood changes just like that and
> you're in a situation when you're at each other's throats."
> *(Perpetrator)*

These perpetrators used the advertising, by means of selective perception, to confirm that it was not their problem and they did not need to feel guilt. For example, they claimed that the violence portrayed in the commercial was extreme and much more severe than they themselves would carry out.

> "It's possible it's slightly exaggerated."
> *(Perpetrator)*

> "It's a wee bit over the top, the lady's face, but I suppose
> you've got to emphasise to people what can be done, so I
> don't suppose it's telling any lies. It would maybe bring
> home to more people that it can go that far."
> *(Perpetrator)*

In addition they felt that the woman in the commercial was passive and not verbally abusive. Again, this was felt to be different from their own experience where it was claimed their partner often provoked them into committing a violent act. This interpretation of events was used to distance the campaign from their own experiences and actions.

> "It seems to be him that's doing all the talking in that way.
> She's not really saying anything, where that doesn't come
> into our circumstances. She's not saying anything at all.
> It's him that's picked on her for some reason."
> *(Perpetrator)*

> "The lady's not saying nothing to him so why is he
> knocking the shit out of her."
> *(Perpetrator)*

These perpetrators were also of the opinion that highlighting the punitive consequences of their actions would not act as a deterrent.

> "What they're saying now basically is, it's a criminal
> offence. No one thinks twice about a criminal offence. It's
> not a deterrent."
> *(Perpetrator)*

4.2.2 Readiness to confront their actions

Those perpetrators who were willing to confront their actions and accepted that they needed help and advice responded to the campaign quite differently from those that sought to deny responsibility for their actions. This group already accepted that they had committed a crime and had experienced shame and remorse. The emotional trauma portrayed in the forty second television commercial tended to bring out and amplify these feelings of shame, remorse and inadequacy. This highlighting of emotions may be considered a valid enough outcome on its own but it should also be noted that this group of perpetrators are prepared to seek out help and support and indeed tend to look to this type of advertising for such support.

Importantly though, the emphasis on the criminal aspect of their behaviour meant there was a reluctance or disincentive to use the support element of the campaign, namely the telephone service, for fear of being reprimanded. In essence it was argued that it would make them *"think twice"* before seeking help.

Paradoxically those perpetrators more predisposed to seeking assistance were not inclined to do so because of the punitive element to the campaign.

Thus, on the one hand, the campaign contributes to a sense of shame but, on the other hand, discourages any efforts to seek support. Indeed it could be argued that it may ultimately result in increased levels of abuse.

This suggests that there is a need for considerable care in combining punitive and supportive elements in one campaign. It also suggests that there is perhaps scope for a campaign which is more 'softly, softly' in its approach and aims to put perpetrators in contact with support services before the violence increases in frequency and severity.

> "Somebody that maybe never went that far, that got into arguments and barnies and maybe never struck her. It might make them think twice about it."
> *(Perpetrator)*

> "It could help people that have not been in our position, that have never been to court."
> *(Perpetrator)*

> "Unless they bring out something similar to this (the programme of support that I'm attending) that violence (portrayed in the commercial) will continue to happen before you get to court."
> *(Perpetrator)*

Indeed it was argued that The Scottish Office campaign should have placed more emphasis on promoting such support services.

> "I think they should have added a wee bit onto that, there's bound to be places you can get help for it, like us. All it tells you is it's a criminal offence."
> *(Perpetrator)*

This was also recognised by sections of the public as an important stage, where the violent behaviour might be curtailed before it escalated. These assumptions would require further research before a campaign strategy could be built around it, but it does suggest a possible way forward for dealing with perpetrators.

Finally, it should be noted that the general public, and victims themselves, often tended to favour a punitive rather than a supportive approach. There was wide agreement with the campaign that the perpetrators should be brought to justice and made to pay for their crimes. Therefore any attempt to provide support for perpetrators may be met with some resistance from these groups, although a support theme for victims was seen to be vital.

This implies that as well as targeting 'pre-habitual' perpetrators, there is potential for a campaign that jointly targets both the victims and the perpetrators, encouraging and supporting them in sorting out their relationship <u>before</u> these difficulties escalate.

Unlike response to the advertising, perpetrators' response to the information service did not vary accordingly to willingness to accept responsibility for their crime. As with the general public, all perpetrators expected the telephone service would provide advice and counselling for people in their situation.

> "There's got to be, obviously somebody at the end of the
> line that's going to give you advice of some description."
> *(Perpetrator)*

There was, therefore, widespread disappointment and condemnation when they learned of the nature of the service on offer.

> "If somebody has gone to all the bother to 'phone you, they
> are obviously looking for advice or help."
> *(Perpetrator)*

> "You tend to listen to an answerphone thing and you go, 'Oh
> to hell with that.'"
> *(Perpetrator)*

Similarly perpetrators did not feel that a pack would have been of use to them at their time of greatest need. Instead personal professional help had been the key to them being able to address their problem .

> "I honestly don't think myself, an information pack would
> be ... you need something like this (programme) or
> somebody to give you advice."
> *(Perpetrator)*

> "I do think you need to talk to somebody more than read it."
> *(Perpetrator)*

4.3 Overview

In terms of indirect effects, perpetrators saw the campaign as part of a general move towards tackling the issue of domestic violence and creating a climate of intolerance. None, however, were aware of it prompting anyone to comment on or address their own violent behaviour.

In terms of direct effects, the findings are more revealing. Given the deep rooted nature of the problem and the subsequent changes in behaviour being sought both in terms of encouraging perpetrators to confront their actions and of providing the support needed to correct this behaviour, the advertising had not, perhaps unsurprisingly, had any observable impact on the perpetrator interviewees. However, the research has demonstrated that advertising may have an intermediate role to play in both facilitating action among immediate family and friends, and in encouraging those perpetrators <u>who recognise</u> that they need support to contact appropriate services. However, at the moment the campaign message and tone do not appear to encourage this. Indeed the punitive element of the campaign may actively discourage perpetrators to seek such support. In addition the support on offer is considered inadequate.

Importantly, a strategy which primarily suggests support to perpetrators is at odds with one which seeks to promote the criminal nature of the behaviour and to stimulate a general climate of abhorrence. The latter approach risks forcing perpetrators further underground and away from any support network. It should also be noted that a more 'softly, softly' approach would not necessarily be consistent with that preferred by the general public, who are more likely to favour a punitive to a preventive strategy. On the other hand, a support message for victims was seen as essential. These factors combine to suggest that if a preventive strategy was adopted it might prove more effective and acceptable if targeting those perpetrators getting 'into' rather than already 'in' difficulty, although the size of this audience group remains unknown. This way it may also prove effective to target victims and perpetrators together, prior to the violence escalating. Such a strategy would require further research.

5.0 THE VICTIMS' PERSPECTIVE

This section explores the victims' perspective. Four focus groups were carried out in West and Central Scotland. These were recruited through Women's Aid (see Section 1.5). It should be noted that only a small proportion of these respondents had been living in an abusive relationship at the time of the campaign. The majority had left their partners and had been living separately for varying periods of time, from a few months to a few years.

First, the victims' response to the problem is outlined (Section 5.1) although, by necessity, it is not a complete analysis of domestic violence. This is followed by an exploration of victims' response to the campaign (Section 5.2).

5.1 Response to the problem

During the discussions, victims gave vivid descriptions of their experiences and patterns of escalating violence.

> "I think it gets worse and worse. The more times you say,
> you take them back and you accept their apologies, the
> worse it gets. They never change."
> *(Victim)*

The sessions revealed a remarkable consistency between the victims' experience and the understanding of the problem shown by the general public. However, although victims described physical violence, they also highlighted mental and sexual abuse which were felt to have a far more demoralising and enduring effect. Sexual abuse was rarely mentioned by the general public groups in the context of domestic violence and their predominant perception was of physical rather than mental abuse.

> "It had always been physical and mental abuse all the time,
> but I didn't realise how bad the mental abuse was until I was
> actually really seriously considering killing the swine."
> *(Victim)*

> "They are like pure animals at times. You had to lie there
> still for them. It (sex) had to be good for them."
> *(Victim)*

> "When my husband was having sex, the more I cried during
> sex, the more pain he inflicted and the more it turned him
> on."
> *(Victim)*

Although they were all living separately from their partners at the time of the interviews, many reported patterns of leaving and returning to their partners more than once. On reflection they often found it difficult to understand why they had endured their partner's abuse, although they had gained some insight now that they were away from the situation.

> "If I had known what it would have been like I would have
> left years ago. I took ten years of it. My husband just didn't
> batter me, my husband used weapons, slashing and God
> knows what."
> *(Victim)*

The turning points for leaving were varied. Some described a realisation that there was no love or warmth left to balance out the fear and violent incidents. Others went further than that, and described seriously considering murdering their partner as the only way out.

> "A few weeks before I left ... it was how can I kill him and get away with it ... Working out how can I do the biggest deed of the lot. Just so I can get peace."
> *(Victim)*

> "Killing the husband can be the only answer they can come to for some women."
> *(Victim)*

> "I'd really have to finish him off. He'd say, 'Well you should hit me back.' Now that's grand, him saying that and he's got a vodka bottle in his hand or a knife or whatever ... with my luck I'd be the one that would kill him."
> *(Victim)*

Others spoke of the pure terror resulting from the excessive violence. The extending of the beatings to their children or the realisation that the children were suffering from the stress of the domestic situation were also cited as a reason for leaving.

> "My turning point was when Calum got hit. He ladled into Calum, and he was only three."
> *(Victim)*

In some instances, it could be a relatively small incident that proved to be the deciding factor.

> "Then one hit or one punch. It's maybe not even as big as the one before, but it's enough. For me, I was absolutely terrified that day."
> *(Victim)*

> "When it gets bad enough you do go. In my situation I just woke up after getting hurt and he was just starting a further assault and there was nothing left anymore - looking at him and it's like hate."
> *(Victim)*

> "I just couldn't take anymore. I mean, I didnae care what anybody says. I think everybody will stand it for so long and there's just the time when you can't take it anymore."
> *(Victim)*

However, despite the physical and emotional harm inflicted upon them, the response of many to the problem while they were in the abusive situation was very much one of inaction. There were a number of reasons for this, which can be broadly grouped around disempowerment, denial and a sense of isolation. These are discussed below.

5.1.1 Disempowerment

Disempowerment evolved in two main areas, emotional and practical. Firstly the continuing physical, verbal and mental abuse often led to a loss of self-esteem and self-respect.

> "Because you start to believe what they say. You start to say to yourself, 'I'm actually good at nothing ...' They don't

even take it out on your body, they take it out on your mind
as well."
(Victim)

In this situation the perpetrator could develop so much power in the relationship that the victim lost control of her own actions and was unable to form her own opinions.

"They take it out on your mind. They've got you so that you
believe what they say."
(Victim)

"I was kind of brainwashed - thick, stupid - you should be
grateful that he wants to look after you."
(Victim)

"You have no say in anything. You cannae do nothing
without consent. You have to account for everything you've
done and where you've been."
(Victim)

Often their partners showed signs of jealousy or insecurity in their anger.

"Or I would put earrings on, 'You're putting earrings on.
Who are you going out to see? No, you must be meeting
someone, you are putting on earrings."
(Victim)

"If you looked at anybody he was on your case. 'Are you
wanting off with him? Is that what you're looking at him
for?'"
(Victim)

Sometimes these pressures would lead to self-blame, where the victim would feel responsible for her partner's actions and that it was, therefore, her responsibility to resolve the problem.

"I was the very devoted woman. I made sure I ironed all his
stuff and his socks, because I thought, you still believe that
it must have been something to do with you."
(Victim)

"Although I know in my heart that it had nothing to do with
me ... there was a part of me believed, 'I must try to do
better with ...'"
(Victim)

The unpredictability of the violence could also be destructive, as even when the woman was not being abused, she would be anticipating the next episode.

"I woke up in the morning and I didn't know if my husband
was going to be in a good mood or a bad mood."
(Victim)

"They're unpredictable. You could say something and he'd
laugh or cuddle you and then say the same thing the
following night and he'd wallop you one."
(Victim)

The victims also described being disempowered in very practical terms in becoming dependent on her partner for all material support such as shelter, clothing and money. The partner often took control of all these areas, not allowing her to make decisions for herself or to take action without permission. If she decided to leave she often had difficulty finding shelter and money to support herself. These problems were compounded by a lack of self-confidence.

> "You actually hear people saying to you, 'Why did you take that?', but you've got to be in the situation yourself to see what you would actually do ... You've got children, a wee baby, where have you got to turn if there's no family?"
> *(Victim)*

> "(After you leave) you are still suffering. You have got years to wait on a house. He is sitting in a big four apartment (house) and you are stuck ... if you knew you could go to a new wee house within six months ... then a lot more people would have the guts to leave."
> *(Victim)*

> "It's the women who have got to move away, not the men."
> *(Victim)*

Many victims still retained some love for their partner in between the violent episodes, and this modified the impetus to leave. In addition, many had been dependent on their partner for providing a 'stable' family background, believing at the time that a two parent family was better than a single parent one.

> "They (others) forget that you are emotionally attached, they forget that you built a relationship up with someone and this was your family unit. If you walk out the door you're breaking up the family unit and there's more things to worry about than you just getting your face smashed in. You've got to think whether you're going to take your kid away from that just for yourself."
> *(Victim)*

5.1.2 Denial

Perhaps surprisingly, victims would make considerable efforts to try and deny the existence of the problem. Thus despite experiencing physical, mental and sexual abuse and, in some cases, quite severe violence, they would deny that abuse was taking place, thus unwittingly supporting the perpetrator. Indeed many of the victims, on reflection, were surprised how their mind had played such tricks. In part this seemed a coping mechanism since an inability to take control of the situation meant that the only way of coping was to deceive oneself into believing that the problem did not exist.

Some also described feeling that they had chosen the perpetrator as their partner, hence leaving him or approaching family or outside agencies for support was an admission of failure and a source of embarrassment.

> "I couldn't ever say what he was doing to me because I felt ashamed. I didn't want to tell anybody what actually happened to me."
> *(Victim)*

> "I think you are ashamed as well, that you are letting them

away with it and you've not done anything about it."
(Victim)

"It's embarrassing as well. It actually challenges - a lot of women don't admit to themselves that the abuse is there."
(Victim)

Denial was also apparent in the way the victim responded to others around her. Victims described repeatedly lying to family and close friends to explain away bruising or illness caused by the violence.

"I don't want to publicise the fact that I've got a bruised eye and be walking into the door because I've got his fist in my face."
(Victim)

"People used to say, 'What a nice fellow that is,' and I'd think, 'Oh, if only you knew,' because you don't go advertising it."
(Victim)

This was often put down to fear of further violence if 'outsiders' interfered or because of shame and embarrassment from admitting the situation. The excuse of *'walking into a door'* was frequently mentioned together with other stories, such as having slipped on a wet floor or having been in a car crash.

"You'll no' even tell your GP. It took me years to tell my GP. The excuse was, 'Oh, the washing machine was leaking.' That was my first beating and he was saying, 'Oh are you sure?' ... and it went on for years."
(Victim)

Thus many victims found themselves in a difficult psychological predicament. In one sense they had to pretend to themselves that the violence was not happening, and in another sense they had to tell deliberate lies to avoid unwanted intervention from their family or those round about them. This could have deeply distorting psychological effects.

5.1.3 Isolation

The factors already discussed had the cumulative effect of isolating the victims from the community and the support they needed. They were often physically isolated in that the perpetrator often controlled when they could leave the house and denied access to family, friends or neighbours.

"I never had any friends. The first thing they take away from you is your mail, you don't have any mail. You cease to be."
(Victim)

"The beatings were getting worse and worse and he's keeping me in the house all the time. He used to lock me up but now he just smacks me in the mouth so I won't go out because my face is black and blue."
(Victim)

> "Or the neighbours think you're a snob because you don't
> talk to them. You spend all your time cleaning the house
> because he's so strict."
> *(Victim)*

They were also perceptually isolated in that they often felt they were the only one experiencing this sort of abuse.

> "Everybody thinks, 'Oh it's just me (being abused).'"
> *(Victim)*

Paradoxically, many also distanced themselves from the idea of being a victim of domestic violence. While admitting that they were treated badly, many sought not to relate their experiences to 'wife battering' but instead saw it as just part of their relationship. This, in part, reflected their own stereotyped image of battered women which had been similar to the general public's perceptions.

> "I actually thought that a battered women had rollers in her
> hair, she had big breasts that flop down to here, she wore an
> apron and she had rolled up socks and no teeth ... There I
> was, a young twenty year old mother holding down a
> responsible job and I was going home at night and I was
> being battered. I was like, 'No, I am not a battered
> woman.'"
> *(Victim)*

In two extreme cases respondents who were being abused had had jobs which involved working with battered women; one worked in a lawyers' office and had taken down statements from abused women and the other worked in a taxi firm where she had dispatched cars to collect women who were escaping from violent situations. At the time, neither of them had related their own experiences to that of the abused women with whom they came in contact.

> "But I wasn't battered as bad. I didn't think I was eligible
> for Women's Aid."
> *(Victim)*

> "I used to work in a taxi office and I just used to think it
> (Women's Aid) was for poor people whose husbands went
> home and hit them. They left for the night and then went
> back the next day."
> *(Victim)*

Their failure to recognise their predicament often meant that victims actually isolated themselves from the support of which they were in dire need.

Many victims went to great lengths to deny the violence they experienced as discussed above. However, where they had recognised a need for help or that need had been apparent to those around them, the response of 'others' to the situation was mixed.

There were mixed feelings about involving the police. While there were generally negative impressions regarding police intervention, the few personal experiences discussed were varied with some finding them helpful and some finding them dismissive.

> "The policeman that came that night when I left. It was him
> that says to me 'You should go to Women's Aid. You don't
> need to put up with this.'"
> *(Victim)*

"My daughter ... the chap she was living with broke into my house, and we called the police. I said, 'Her ex-boyfriend did it' and the policeman turned round and says to my daughter, 'Now you brought it on yourself didn't you?' (one year ago)."
(Victim)

"We had somebody recently, the police came round and they were told to sort it out themselves."
(Victim)

In addition it was expected that calling in the police could have serious potential consequences for the victim, both in the short and long term.

"Many women, if they mention the police, they'll get a doing for it, if they do call the police they'll get a doing for it as soon as he's let out."
(Victim)

"If they go to court they get fined and you're struggling to pay the fine off the house-keeping money."
(Victim)

Similarly among family, friends and neighbours response had varied. Some had been helpful.

"My parents were brilliant. They just got me right out (when the partner was violent)!"
(Victim)

"I never spoke to my neighbours and yet my neighbour used to call the police every Friday or Saturday night. I couldn't even say, 'Thanks very much', ... because I knew if I spoke to them I could get into trouble ... obviously she realised it was embarrassing and never pushed."
(Victim)

In some instances, however, where the victim had approached others for help, the support was not forthcoming. Thus help was sometimes refused when requested or the victim was told to put up with the situation. In some cases the perpetrator was defended, especially by his own family. Such lack of support, and even rejection, would add to the victim's sense of isolation and powerlessness.

"One night when he was being really violent - it was sticks, you know - I couldn't get in touch with my mum ... I went and ran next door (I thought we were really friendly) and I'll never forget, the two of them came to the door and I said, 'Look, you need to do something, he is going off his head in there, he is going crazy.' The two of them looked at each other and says, 'Sorry, we don't want to get involved.'"
(Victim)

"Whether your mum or dad liked the fellow you were going to marry or not. All they tell you was 'You married him. You made your bed, you lie it it. Don't come crawling to me.'"
(Victim)

> "And you don't want to break up the family, especially if you've got wee ones. Your family are saying certain things like, 'You married him.' I was told to put up with it and that's going through your head."
> *(Victim)*

> "My mother-in-law once said to me, 'That's what is up with him. He has a high sex drive,' and if I just gave him a bit more (sex), everything would be fine."
> *(Victim)*

Despite the fact that help may not be forthcoming, victims were uncertain about what recommendations they could make to improve the situation and to encourage effective support from the public. Importantly, they felt that different types of intervention were appropriate for different situations and hence, that some interventions, while potentially helpful, could also be inappropriate and even counter-productive.

In the light of these findings, the main need that emerged for those victims outwith the support networks, was to encourage them to recognise that they have a common problem and that although individual patterns may vary, what they are experiencing <u>is</u> domestic violence and as such is unacceptable. This is only likely to be effective where appropriate solutions to their problems in the form of advice, help and support are made available. Raising expectations and then failing to deliver is likely to have a counter-productive effect.

5.2   Response to the campaign

The campaign was generally welcomed by the victims. However, further discussion revealed some difficulties with the material. The range of responses are discussed below in terms of the victims' perceptions of the potential response by the three main target groups; the general public, perpetrators and the victims themselves.

5.2.1 Victims' perceptions of the general public's response

The victims felt that the campaign gave recognition to their problem. As such, they felt it could raise awareness and interest among the general public whom they felt did not fully understand the issue.

> "So maybe that's one of the good things about it. Maybe it will make neighbours a bit more aware."
> *(Victim)*

In doing so, it was believed that it might contribute to a climate of intolerance and ultimately diminish the acceptability surrounding domestic violence, fuelling concern for its victims.

> "Hopefully it will make the public wonder if they know anybody that's been abused."
> *(Victim)*

It was recognised however, that it did not give guidance on how to help, although it did promote an information service which was recognised and welcomed in principal.

5.2.2 Victims' perceptions of the perpetrators' response

It was believed that the campaign could have provoked perpetrators to question their actions. However, it was felt that its effectiveness in achieving this would be dependent on the perpetrator's mood and personal circumstances.

> "It would depend what kind of a mood he was in when he
> was watching it. He wasnae violent all the time."
> *(Victim)*

It should be noted that these victims had been through prolonged and extremely difficult experiences and had little expectation of their violent partner reforming.

There was also recognition that the problem could not be solved by communication alone but required extensive psychological support and counselling. Victims were not aware of such services for perpetrators, but were supportive of the concept and felt they should be developed and actively promoted.

> "But there's no number at the end to say, 'Look, if you're
> being abusive towards your partner, call up.' Because in his
> saner moments he used to say, 'Can you not even contact
> Women's Aid to find out if there's a number I can go to?'
> Ten minutes later he'd smack me in the mouth."
> *(Victim)*

> "You never know - I work in the shop (Women's Aid fund-
> raising) and I had a man coming in asking me if there was a
> place where they helped battered men, and his face was all
> ..."
> *(Victim)*

It was acknowledged that some men might contemplate seeking help, perhaps in the early stages of an abusive relationship.

> "Some of these men might be doing it (telephoning the
> service) because there's something wrong with them and
> they are realising."
> *(Victim)*

There was also some evidence of counter-productive effects of the campaign, although these were rarely reported during the discussions. Only two women had been in abusive relationships since the campaign was launched. One of these victims described how the screening of the forty second television commercial had actually triggered a violent attack. She described how her partner had said, *"I suppose you think that's smart"* and then proceeded to beat her. As a result she lived in fear of the commercial being screened when they were both in the room. She had experienced similar problems with other media coverage of the issue and had, in the past, hidden magazines which had articles on domestic violence, and regularly checked the newspapers for any coverage of the issue to avoid triggering an attack.

> "(It's) unfortunate if you live in an abusive relationship
> because every time it's shown on the TV then they blame
> you and you end up getting smacked yourself ... It got to
> the bit where I was scared to watch TV ... you get angry
> with the adverts. The first time the advert was on he said, 'I
> suppose you think that's smart'. I'm all for the campaign
> now that I'm away from it all but it's all these women that
> are scared for the TV. I've never been so terrified in my
> life."

(Victim)

Other victims recognised that this could be a potential problem. In particular, it was felt that the initial screening during the World Cup could have exacerbated the situation if the perpetrator objected to his viewing being interrupted or if he was angry as a result of his team losing.

> "It's been aimed at men and it works, it gets them. Unfortunately, we get it as well. It does work, it thingmys their conscience."
> *(Victim)*

> "It could actually have a negative effect on women sitting in their home being abused at that point because it could be them in an hours time if the team didn't win."
> *(Victim)*

Conversely, it was also recognised that perpetrators might deny that the campaign related to them, reflecting their perception of a more generalised pattern of denial of the violence, which was in fact apparent among the perpetrators interviewed (see Section 4.2.1). It was believed that the severity of the physical damage, together with the focus on physical abuse, could result in perpetrators distancing themselves from the commercial and its message. The other victim who had seen the commercial while living in an abusive relationship described her boyfriend's response:

> "It didnae have any effect on my boyfriend. It wasnae important. (As far as he was concerned) it was nothing to do with him"
> *(Victim)*

While another reported the following experience;

> "One of the women that's in the Refuge said (that her partner said), 'Well you ought to be thankful I don't make your face look like that.' He just did it on the body, 'At least you cannae see it.' (She) can't walk but ... (her face is not marked)."
> *(Victim)*

5.2.3 Victims' response

There was broad support for the campaign among victims. This was primarily based upon a belief that their problem was not widely recognised by the authorities, hence the campaign was a means of raising awareness and reassuring victims that their predicament was receiving attention

> "I think it would help. 'God, not just me that is getting that.' And also it would help people who didn't think that was going on at all."
> *(Victim)*

However, victims were also critical of the campaign. These criticisms are examined in relation to the campaign's two main component parts: first, the awareness raising component, focussing on the forty second television commercial and the 'Love and Hate' outdoor poster; and, secondly, the information giving component, focussing on the ten second commercial and the associated telephone line and information pack.

(i)   Response to the awareness raising component

The forty second television commercial was found by many to be upsetting. The screaming and shouting was frequently mentioned and many found the bruising on the victim's face difficult to look at.

> "I couldn't even look at it. It brings it all back. You thought
> you could forget about what happened to you but when you
> see that you think 'Oh'!"
> *(Victim)*

Viewing the commercial often reminded them of their own experiences, resulting in a very personal interpretation of what was taking place.

> "Very realistic, especially when you know what the screams
> are for."
> *(Victim)*

> "You feel as though you've been in the same situation. The
> screams make you think, well me personally, I feel as
> though he's going to hit me more. That's what I went
> through and the effect is the only one that affects me ...
> hearing that and the woman reacting to that situation."
> *(Victim)*

The 'Love and Hate' poster also reminded some of their experiences and could be upsetting.

Importantly, these reactions did not diminish the victims' support for the campaign and the need to raise awareness of the issue.

Further discussions however, revealed some detailed concerns with the material. The way in which domestic violence was portrayed raised many questions regarding, for example, the form of violence inflicted on the victim and the choice of setting.

The extensive bruising on the victim's face was not considered to be typical. It was felt that physical abuse was normally targeted at the victim's body where it could not be seen by others.

> "It's very rarely they mark your face. It shows the side the
> public want to see. If a woman is abused as bad as that
> physically then she'll stay in the house until ... (it's
> cleared)."
> *(Victim)*

This raised doubts about whether victims would identify with the campaign and was particularly significant given the problem of denial described above. Many argued that the extensive nature of the injuries would further discourage identification.

> "My worry from the adverts is that when I was being
> battered I couldn't come to terms that I was a battered
> woman."
> *(Victim)*

> "A lot of women (ringing Women's Aid) were saying,
> 'Well, I'm not as bad as her on the television so maybe I'm
> not that bad.' And we were having to say to them, 'If there
> is physical violence, you should come and seek help."
> *(Victim)*

> "People that are getting a different kind of violence (would say) 'Maybe I can't go and get help from them because he is hitting her face but I am not getting that.'"
>   *(Victim)*

Many concluded this particular debate on a more positive note, agreeing that showing bruising on the body was problematic in a mass media campaign and expressing the hope that future initiatives would be able to highlight the wide range of abuse inflicted on victims.

> "Why don't they show it in the house? When the house gets wrecked. The smashing furniture ... when you are standing ironing and you are not ironing the right shirt. The kids are crying and he can't watch TV ... and the dinner is not on the table."
>   *(Victim)*

> "Show a whole half hour programme with wee bits in it ... someone getting raped in a marriage ... mental and verbal abuse ... to let them see that there is more than one way a man can abuse a woman."
>   *(Victim)*

Concern was also expressed by some victims over the choice of setting. The pub was seen to be inadvertently implying that alcohol was the cause of domestic violence where, in reality, violence could occur without the presence of alcohol.

> "Well see the ad, it's all about being in the pub and it's drink right? Battered women don't (always) get battered through drink, they (also) do it when they are sober ... I put up with about eight years of domestic violence and blamed it on alcohol ... (after leaving) I realised alcohol was only a catalyst."
>   *(Victim)*

It was widely believed that domestic violence was often calculated rather than impulsive and that the reference to alcohol distorted the malicious nature of the crime.

In addition to the two main concerns, a range of minor executional issues were raised. These did not arouse the same degree of concern. First, it was felt that an abused woman would not be permitted to go to the pub, especially on her own.

> "You are not allowed to go into the pub for a drink anyway. You wouldn't be in a pub."
>   *(Victim)*

> "In my experience I would say they were old partners because she couldn't have walked into a pub on her own, not if they were together."
>   *(Victim)*

Secondly, the victim was felt to be passive. This, combined with the male voice-over, led to a feeling that the woman did not have a voice in the commercial.

> "The whole way through the woman is very passive, it's just her face, the violence has been done to her. The whole talking is done again by a man right through the ad ... so

again it's not generally giving women a voice."
(Victim)

"I sit there and I go, 'Hit him. Hit him (to the woman).' I want to skelp him, where I couldn't hit my husband."
(Victim)

Finally, concern was expressed by a few respondents that elements of the campaign tended to promote the traditional perpetrator stereotype. This was epitomised by the 'Love and Hate' poster.

"A lot of other comments about the ad are that it is portraying a certain type of man, especially the knuckles one. It's very forceful that love and hate ... It's a macho hard man from the east end of Glasgow or the housing estate ... It's not saying this could be a lawyer or a doctor."
(Victim)

(ii) *Response to the information giving component*

As with the perpetrators and the general public, the ten second television commercial was widely criticised on the grounds that it was likely to have raised expectations of help and support which were not ultimately met. Like the general public, the victims' assumed the commercial was promoting a telephone counselling service.

All victims expressed amazement that the service comprised a recorded message linked to the distribution of an information pack and were dismissive of its value. They envisaged, like the general public (see Section 3.3), that the telephone service was most likely to be used in times of acute distress when practical and emotional support were both essential.

"That's no good. Because when you run you could be running for your life because you know he battered you before. 'Cos I grabbed my weans and ran ... I ran out in my nightgown."
(Victim)

In addition, victims highlighted the practical problems of having a pack sent to a caller, where it could be difficult for the victim to keep it hidden from her partner.

"You would need to have it hidden from your partner, and then it's finding the time to read it to see how it can help you. And then if you can't (read it) then there's no point in having it."
(Victim)

One episode described was of a well meaning outsider contacting the information line. A pack had subsequently been sent to the victim's house, with potentially violent repercussions.

"Somebody phoned the office and (said) she got a pack which somebody else had sent away for and luckily she picked up the post that day and opened it herself. If her man had opened it she would really have been absolutely for it."
(Victim)

Victims also confirmed that it was difficult to provide an alternative address as those being abused were unlikely to have close friends they could regularly visit and often they would deny the existence of the abuse to others.

63

"There's no way you could have that in the house. He would find it. And even if you did know somebody (to send it to) it's getting out to go to that somebody to read it, and you wouldn't be allowed to do that either."
(Victim)

Doubts were also expressed over the quality of the advice given in the information pack, in particular, whether 'walking away' from a fight was realistic.

"I could have laughed there when I read 'Agree with your partner in advance ...' When he was sober he would say 'The next time I'm going to drink too much stop me. Say to me 'You've had enough' and I'll agree with you!' So he would start his fourth or fifth pint and I would say to him, 'Excuse me love, you said I was to tell you' ... and you would land back in the chair."
(Victim)

Victims also doubted whether perpetrators would use the pack if encouraged to do so by the victim or other close family members or friends.

"I think if the woman sent away for it, the man wouldn't be interested in it."
(Victim)

Despite these strong criticisms, victims were not wholly dismissive of using a freephone service providing it delivered personal professional advice and access to appropriate counselling and support. However, as a method of delivering support even telephoning for help carried risks.

"I remember he tried to break my hands with the 'phone one night because I was 'phoning for help. 'I'll stop you using the 'phone,' and it was slapped down on my hands."
(Victim)

It is also important to note that the perceived failure of the campaign's information component to adequately meet the expectations the campaign as a whole is likely to have raised, provoked considerable discussion about the use of resources and the ability of existing services to meet any subsequent increase in demand.

"We were getting a lot of mothers 'phoning up, 'My daughter, I've watched the advert, I know it's happening, can I bring her down.' We're getting a lot of aunties, grandmothers coming forward."
(Victim)

"In a lot of ways it highlights Women's Aid. It can be positive, but it still comes down to how much does it cost for the campaign. That's what annoys me ... it's saying call somebody but if they are not going to find anybody to answer ..."
(Victim)

"On the other hand the money that was spent of the campaign could have been put towards refuges and women's groups that needed the money to survive."
(Victim)

These discussions focussed concern on the integrity of The Scottish Office campaign.

> "I'm hoping they don't sweep it under the carpet after they
> have put out one (campaign) ... It's all well and good
> preaching, but what happens once they've finished it (the
> campaign)."
> *(Victim)*

> "They should be supporting the refuges and the women who
> are working there. They shouldn't just give us advertising
> and nothing else."
> *(Victim)*

5.3 Overview

Victims gave vivid descriptions of their experiences of living with their abusive partner. Many of the aspects highlighted were also mentioned by the general public respondents, suggesting that the public at large had considerable awareness of the issues around domestic violence, albeit not at a personal level.

The victims experiences incorporated physical, mental and sexual abuse, with patterns of ongoing and escalating violence. However, they found it difficult to identify the kind of help that would be beneficial for victims and it was felt that the nature of effective support would vary with different situations and there could not be a blanket recommendation for appropriate interventions.

There was broad support among victims for campaigning on the issue and for this campaign in particular.

However, there were some criticisms of some aspects of the campaign. In particular, it was felt that it did not portray the wide range of physical, mental and sexual abuse that could be experienced by women. In addition, the extensive bruising on the victim's face was considered to be atypical of physical abuse, which was felt to be normally targeted at the victim's body where it could not be seen by others. Importantly, it was suggested that the location, the overtly physical portrayal and the extreme nature of the injuries might discourage those in abusive relationships from personally identifing with the campaign.

Concern was also expressed over the setting of the commercial in a pub, since this was seen to imply that alcohol was the cause of domestic violence when, in reality, violence often occured without the presence of alcohol.

Members of the victims' group were also highly critical of the ten second follow-up commercial and the telephone information line, for similar reasons to those identified by memebers of the general public. It was also felt that having an information pack sent to the caller might cause considerable practical difficulties or even result in further domestic violence.

However, the key issue to emerge upon developing a fuller appreciation of what the campaign had to offer, was a need to address any expectations raised by the campaign through appropriate follow-up and support. In addition, it ws felt that attention needed to be given to the way domestic violence was portrayed in the awareness raising component of the campaign.

6.0 SUMMARY AND CONCLUSIONS

6.1 Summary

6.1.1 Perceptions and experiences of domestic violence

There was considerable understanding of the issues relating to domestic violence among the general public. Domestic violence was seen to be distinct from the tensions, disputes and occasional fights which were part of a 'normal' relationship. It was seen to be ongoing and to escalate, becoming more frequent and malicious. It was primarily seen to incorporate physical violence, but mental abuse was also seen to be significant The issues highlighted were consistent with those described by victims, indicating the validity of public perceptions. Among the general public, and also the victim and perpetrator groups, there was little expectation of habitual abusers reforming without considerable support, although there was believed to be some potential for change in the early stages of the situation. Victims also found difficulty in breaking away from the pattern of domestic violence, gradually becoming disempowered and isolated, while still denying the abuse was taking place.

The issue aroused an emotional response from the general public, with empathy for the victims combined with incredulity that they remained in the relationship. While objectively all domestic violence was seen to be unacceptable, there were indications that some aspects might be less readily condemned.

Although members of the public expressed considerable concern for victims, there was also uncertainty about how to respond if one became aware of an abusive situation. Uncertainty was expressed over how to determine whether the situation was indeed abusive and whether and what intervention would be appropriate. This mismatch between the desire to act and the inability to determine an appropriate course of action, led to a sense of powerlessness and resulted in apathy and ultimately tolerance.

6.1.2 Response to the campaign

There was high awareness of The Scottish Office campaign among all three target groups. It aroused considerable interest in the subject area and has been especially valuable in this respect in those areas, such as the West of Scotland, where existing campaigning (such as Zero Tolerance) has been less extensive.

The forty second television commercial was the element of the campaign most often recalled. It built on existing awareness of the issue by bringing it into focus in a powerful and dramatic way. It aroused the intended emotions of abhorrence and condemnation and also provided new information about the criminality of domestic violence to those less well informed. Victims were particularly supportive of this element of the campaign, although it did not always provoke the desired reaction among perpetrators, with the severe nature of the portrayal resulting in a disassociation from the message. Indeed, there was also some evidence that victims currently in an abusive situation could fail to identify with the commercial for the same reasons. There were also concerns raised about the way it portrayed domestic violence, for example, the atypical location of the facial bruising, the perceived severity of the injury and the perceived link between the crime and alcohol which was seen to misrepresent the violence as not malicious. In addition, although the commercial encouraged the general public to consider a situation of which they had limited experience, it did not challenge them to act in relation to domestic violence, nor did it give guidance on what interventions were appropriate in such situations.

Other aspects of the campaign were less well received. There was limited awareness of the ten second commercial, while the support services it promoted, namely the information line, telephone message and information pack, were not seen to be appropriate to the needs of potential users. It was commonly anticipated that callers, particularly victims, would be in an emotional state and that a personal counselling service would be required to address their needs. Finally while the 'Love and Hate' outdoor poster had impact, the message was not understood and it was seen to portray a stereotypical 'working class' image of perpetrators which was inconsistent with other media messages being promoted at the time of the campaign.

6.2   Conclusions

Viewed from a strategic perspective it is clear that the three target groups, namely the general public, victims and perpetrators, have different needs and therefore require different forms of support. Significantly, although there is potential to develop a media based campaign for the general public, it was evident that the needs of perpetrators and victims are more complex, and for campaigns to be effective there is a need to provide appropriate follow-up and support. In effect, with perpetrators and victims it is perhaps more appropriate to view the media as an intermediary, raising awareness, arousing interest and facilitating access to appropriate support services. In this sense, where behaviour patterns are deep-rooted and difficult to change, as is the case with domestic violence, the media has a role to play as part of a wider package of support.

When using the mass media it is also important to consider the impacts (intended or otherwise) on all the groups who might be affected by the initiative; in this case not just the general public but also the victims and perpetrators. In this respect it is worth noting that the main forty second television commercial was highly successful in raising the profile of domestic violence among the public but the dramatic images used to achieve this could at the same time have the effect of triggering a violent attack.

Given these strategic considerations, the conclusions now examine the needs of the three target groups separately and the role that the media might play in addressing these.

6.2.1   The general public

The considerable interest aroused by The Scottish Office campaign provides an ideal platform for a campaign designed specifically to generate greater public involvement in the issue. There is scope for at least two approaches here.

First, despite an underlying willingness to take action, the public lack the necessary knowledge and experience to react effectively in situations of domestic violence; largely because of the private nature of the crime, they are often unaware of what potential actions exist and when each might be appropriate.

Thus there is potential for a campaign to give the public guidance on how to actively address the issue and, in so doing, to minimise the number currently ignoring it and subsequently contributing to a counter-climate of tolerance. Questions that need addressing include; how should I react? When should I telephone the police? When should I contact the support services? When should I get involved in trying to break up an argument? When should I approach the victim and offer support?

Importantly, such an approach would need to recognise the variety of situations that might occur and that a standard response might prove inappropriate. Victims themselves recalled the varying appropriateness of involvement or non-involvement of others and agreed that what might be useful in one set of circumstances might not be useful in another. They themselves found it difficult to make general recommendations about specific courses of action.

Secondly, there is potential for a number of information based campaigns. One option is to address the conflicting perceptions about the criminal nature of domestic violence. On the one hand, there was widespread acceptance that domestic violence is a crime but on the other hand it is inconsistent with the underlying perception that the police and courts do not address the problem effectively. For example, the police were seen to treat such incidents as 'domestics' rather than as assaults. Within this area there is scope for promoting the more caring and proactive role of the police.

There is also potential for more confrontational campaign messages which focus, not upon the dramatic and indisputable areas of domestic violence, but which look at the less clearly understood areas. Initiatives here could usefully deal with those actions which either condone or encourage tolerance of domestic violence; for example, ignoring the apparent occurrence of domestic violence or failing to confront light-hearted comments made in casual conversation which provide tacit approval for such violence. Such comments were observed in the early stages of the research.

6.2.2 Victims

The victims who took part in the research responded favourably to the campaign. Many felt it gave recognition to their problem and was supportive of those victims currently living in violent relationships. However, given the private nature of the experience, victims typically try to keep the abuse secret, denying its existence to both themselves and others. Thus, when communicating directly with victims, there is a need to use images and messages to which they can readily relate if they are to recognise the support networks as a solution to their predicament. It is important to encourage victims outwith existing networks to recognise that although individual patterns may vary, what they are experiencing is domestic violence and as such is unacceptable. In addition, this is only likely to be effective when appropriate solutions in the form of support services are provided. Finally, with this group especially, raising expectations of support and then failing to deliver is likely to have a counter-productive effect.

6.2.3 Perpetrators

Perpetrators were aware of the campaign and acknowledged it as contributing to the growing climate of disapproval of domestic violence. However, none reported the campaign prompting anyone to comment directly on their own violent behaviour or encouraging them to address it themselves.

Evidence suggests that the deep-rooted nature of the behaviour and the profound behaviour changes being sought means that communication initiatives on their own are likely to have a limited impact. In addition, there were elements of The Scottish Office campaign which mitigated against effectiveness with the target audience. In particular, the punitive element of the campaign, although stimulating shame and guilt among some perpetrators, actively discourages these same perpetrators to use the support on offer. The research indicates that those perpetrators who are prepared to confront their behaviour are also predisposed to respond to offers of support. These findings suggest that a campaign with a substantive support element, adopting a more conciliatory tone, may prove more effective with this perpetrator sub-group. Perpetrators who demonstrate patterns of denial are likely, however, to prove less responsive to both offers of support and attempts to generate negative emotions such as guilt and shame.

Campaigns which are seen primarily to support perpetrators would not be consistent with that preferred by the general public, who tended to favour a punitive strategy. Similarly, appearing to support perpetrators at the expense of victims would be unacceptable. Evidence suggests that targeting perpetrators getting 'into' rather that already 'in' difficulty, would be both more effective and acceptable to the wider public than targeting habitual abusers. Indeed, such a strategy could involve targeting both victims and perpetrators together, prior to the violence escalating. This route would require further research.

CAMPAIGN MATERIALS

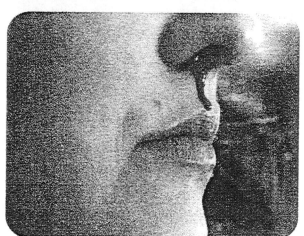

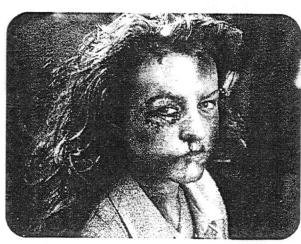
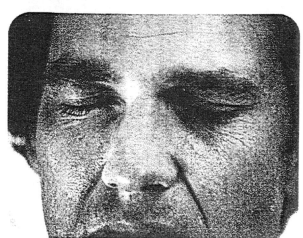

10" TV COMMERCIAL

WE'RE ALL SORRY DOMESTIC VIOLENCE HAPPENS.

BUT BEING SORRY WON'T CHANGE ANYTHING.

PHONE 0800 33 66 99 IF YOU'RE A VICTIM, AN OFFENDER, OR KNOW SOMEONE WHO IS.

WHICH ONE WILL YOU GIVE HER TONIGHT?

DOMESTIC VIOLENCE IS A CRIMINAL OFFENCE. WHEN WILL YOU FACE UP TO IT?

THE SCOTTISH OFFICE

DISCUSSION BRIEF FOR GROUP DISCUSSIONS

'Warm-up' discussion

- <u>Introduction</u>: Relationships are never perfect .../living with someone, although it often has many benefits, inevitably has some stresses and strains, tensions and conflicts, some large, some minor ..../can we kick-off by talking about....

  - type of pressures you typically deal with (adopt a light-hearted tone).
  - how you cope with these.
  - how do you learn and cope about these things.
  - would you ever seek advice/when/who from/under what circumstances/how go about it.
  - why only in these situations (explore private/public domain).
  - importance attached to non-personal sources of information.
  - what about official sources of information and advice - who/under what circumstances.
  - what about the police/social work - what is their role in this type of area.

Perceptions of violence in the domestic situation

- Perceived types/range of violence (images, scenarios, visualisations).

- How people define and distinguish between different types and severity.

- Perceptions of causes and effects of violence.

- Perceptions of general trends and incidence of domestic violence (follow up with response to validity of some of Zero Tolerance statements). Perceived influences/sources.

- Discussion of domestic violence - context/networks.

- Perceived value of media publicity on the issue.

Perceived proximity to domestic violence

- Awareness of it occuring among people known to them eg. social or work place networks.

- Indirect or direct experiences (personal experiences will <u>only</u> be probed where information is volunteered. One-to-one discussion after the group session will be considered if more appropriate).

- Perceived ability/willingness to take action about domestic violence. What action?

Perceptions of response of public institutions, society and individuals

- Knowledge of, and attitudes towards, legal aspects and policing of the problem.

    - eg. criminality of domestic assault
    - eg. response of police to a call out
    - information and information sources

- Knowledge of related initiatives.

    - eg. Woman's Aid, male perpetrator groups
    - role of these initiatives
    - how to contact them

- Perceptions of individual ability to take action. What sort of action and why not.

    - victim
    - perpetrator
    - on-looker, eg. neighbour, relative, workmate

Response to the concept of public campaigns on this issue

- Perceived coverage of the issue (content/extent/gaps).

- Values attached to such campaigns.

- Ways in which it should be portrayed.

- Message(s) to be given - issues/accuracy.

Response to the Scottish Office campaign*

- For each commercial:

    ie. 40 second and 10 second - posters in later groups.

    - perceived target - identification/exclusion
    - perceived message
    - executional details
    - perceived source

- Helpline

    - expectations from the Helpline
    - perceived user
    - response to the pack. Likes/dislikes.

- Comparisons will be sought with other campaigns, eg. Zero Tolerance.

* The research will pick up on earlier issues discussed as appropriate.

DOMESTIC VIOLENCE MEDIA CAMPAIGN

QUANTITATIVE EVALUATION

**Main findings from a two-stage research exercise
carried out by System Three Scotland**

NOTE

Tables showing full results of both stages of the System Three Scotland research, broken down by a number of key demographic variables, are available on request from:

> The Central Research Unit
> Criminological Research Branch
> Room 306 St Andrew's House
> Regent Road
> Edinburgh EH1 3DG

Aims and method

The research by System Three Scotland was intended to examine the impact and effectiveness of the campaign in terms of awareness and understanding among the adult population of Scotland. It was carried out in two phases - one conducted shortly after the initial burst of television campaigning, the second towards the end of the year once the campaigning had run its course. The research was carried out as part of System Three Scotland's monthly Omnibus, the Scottish Opinion Survey. For both stages a quota sampling method was employed to select and interview just over a thousand adults aged 16 and over in their own homes. To ensure that the samples were representative of the adult population of Scotland in terms of age, sex and class, they were weighted to match population estimates from the National Readership Survey of July 1992-June 1993.

Awareness of the campaign

At the first stage of monitoring, the Scottish Office campaign had only run on television, although there had been some coverage of the campaign launch in the press. However, some local authorities had also been running the 'Zero Tolerance' poster campaign and responses to questions about awareness of poster advertising at the first stage of monitoring undoubtedly reflect this.

Spontaneous awareness

Respondents were asked whether they had seen any advertising at all recently on the subject of domestic violence. Responses from both stages of the research are shown below.

Table 1
Spontaneous recall of advertising on the subject of domestic violence

%	Stage 1	Stage 2
At all	84	82
Television	81	75
Posters	7	16
Newspapers	7	10
Magazines	1	2
Cinema	-	1
Other	2	5
Seen, don't know where	1	1
n (unweighted)	1058	1044

The initial burst of television activity achieved an exceptionally high level of impact in being recalled spontaneously by more than 8 in 10 respondents (81%). Spontaneous recall of television advertising was slightly lower in Stage 2, after intermittent showings of the commercial during the autumn - nevertheless, at 75%, it remains very high. Moreover, awareness of poster advertising on domestic violence rose from 7% in Stage 1 to 16% in Stage 2. While this may, in part, relate to the Zero Tolerance campaign, it is highly likely that this also reflects the poster element of the Scottish Office campaign.

Prompted recognition of the television campaign

In order to establish the overall reach of the television campaign at each stage, respondents were shown a photo-prompt relating to the 40-second commercial and asked whether they recalled having seen it on television. This produced even higher levels of awareness - 91% of respondents at Stage 1 reporting having seen the commercial and 89% at Stage 2. At each stage, at least 82% in all demographic and geographic sub-groups had seen the commercial and, at Stage 2, 97% of 16-24 year olds had done so - an extraordinarily high figure.

Reactions to the campaign

To probe respondents' reactions to the television commercial, Stage 1 of the research employed a series of agree-disagree statements relating to the message of the campaign and overall attitudes towards it.

Understanding of the main message of the campaign

As Table 2 shows, there was strong agreement on the first two statements relating to the message of the television commercial. Thus, almost two thirds of respondents agreed strongly that the commercial was trying to show that a man who beats his partner can be prosecuted and that domestic violence usually takes place behind closed doors.

Table 2
Messages communicated by the television advertisement (Stage 1)

(%) n (unweighted)=961	Agree Strongly	Agree Slightly	Neither agree nor disagree	Disagree slightly	Disagree strongly	Don't Know	Mean Score[*]
The ad is trying to say that a man who beats his partner can be prosecuted	63	25	3	5	2	2	1.45
The ad is trying to say that domestic violence takes place behind closed doors	64	27	2	3	1	2	1.52
The ad is trying to say that domestic violence is related to drinking alcohol	28	34	6	20	10	1	0.51
The ad is trying to say that only men who beat up their partners very badly are breaking the law	14	16	3	22	42	2	-0.64

[*] Mean scores are based on a five point rating scale from 'agree strongly'=+2 to 'disagree strongly'=-2.

Opinion on the other two statements was less clear cut, however, suggesting a certain amount of confusion resulting from elements of the commercial's storyline. Three in 10 respondents (30%) agreed (either strongly or slightly) that 'only men who beat up their partners very badly are breaking the law', reflecting the fact that the physical abuse shown in the commercial was of an extreme nature. This figure increased with age. A majority of respondents (62%) also agreed with the statement that 'domestic violence is related to drinking alcohol', which is clearly the result of the advertisement being set in a pub. Again, this view was more common among older respondents and among those from lower socio-economic groups.

Table 3
Interpretation of the advertisement as portraying domestic violence as related to the consumption of alcohol (Stage 1)

	AGE				CLASS			
	16-24	25-34	35-54	55+	AB	C1	C2	DE
Agree	44	59	64	72	57	61	62	65
Disagree	45	35	28	21	35	32	29	27
n (unweighted)	129	220	324	288	132	236	274	319

There was very little difference in interpretation of the commercial between men and women.

General attitudes towards the commercial

Attitudes towards the commercial and its perceived effectiveness were again explored through the use of agree-disagree statements.

Table 4
General attitudes towards the television advertisement (Stage 1)

(%) n (Unweighted)=961	Agree Strongly	Agree Slightly	Neither agree nor disagree	Disagree slightly	Disagree strongly	Don't Know	Mean Score[*]
The campaign has told me something new	9	21	7	26	35	1	-0.56
This will not stop men who are violent towards their partners	41	27	4	14	11	3	+0.75
It certainly makes you think about domestic violence	59	32	3	4	2	1	+1.43
It does not show domestic violence realistically	11	19	10	25	30	5	-0.47
The campaign is just a waste of money	5	5	3	20	65	2	-1.39

[*] Mean scores are based on a five point rating scale from 'agree strongly'=+2 to 'disagree strongly'=-2.

As Table 4 shows, there was widespread agreement among respondents (91%) that the commercial 'certainly makes you think about domestic violence', suggesting that the campaign was at least partially effective in raising the profile of the issue. The commercial appears to have had less impact in terms of educating viewers, with just 30% agreeing that it had told them something new. There was also some scepticism about the impact of the commercial on male perpetrators, with over two-thirds of respondents (68%) agreeing that it would not stop men who are violent towards their partners. A minority (30%) also felt that the portrayal of domestic violence in the commercial was unrealistic.

Despite these reservations, however, there appears to be broad public support for the campaign - while 10% of respondents agreed that the campaign was 'just a waste of money', 65% disagreed 'strongly' with the same statement. Younger respondents were much more likely to disagree with the suggestion that the campaign had been a waste of money.

General attitudes towards domestic violence

A further battery of agree-disagree statements was used to probe respondents' attitudes towards domestic violence in general. Although these questions were included at both stages of the research, it should be emphasised that this was not a pre- and post-advertising monitor, since both stages were carried out subsequent to a burst of television advertising and similar proportions of respondents (89% and 91%) had seen the television campaign at each point.

As Table 5 indicates, for a number of the statements, attitudes remained very stable across the two stages of the research. The results for Stage 2 are shown below, with Stage 1 results in brackets:

- 74% **disagreed** that domestic violence is not a common occurrence in Scotland (76%)

- 72% **disagreed** that violence in private between partners is nobody's business but their own (69%)

- 89% **agreed** that there should be more services provided for those suffering from domestic violence (88%)

- 92% **agreed** that men who hit their partners can be prosecuted in court (92%)

As Table 5 shows, however, there were some developments on some of the other issues covered. While there was no overall shift in the overall mean scores on the question of whether men can sometimes have a good reason for hitting their partners, the percentage disagreeing with this point of view did increase from 77% to 81%. On the other hand, there was some softening of attitudes relating to the perceived illegality of violence of this kind. The percentage of respondents agreeing that it was only cases in which one partner is badly beaten up which are against the law increased from 16% to 21%; and, although the overall percentage agreeing that men who hit their partners can be prosecuted in court remained unchanged at 92%, there was a sharp fall-off in the level of 'strong' agreement from 74% to 60%. This movement was spread across the sample rather than concentrated in any particular subgroups.

Table 5
General attitudes towards domestic violence (Stages 1&2)

(%) n (unweighted): Stage 1=1058 Stage 2=1044		Agree Strongly	Agree Slightly	Neither agree nor disagree	Disagree slightly	Disagree strongly	Don't Know	Mean Score *
Domestic violence is not a common occurrence in Scotland	Stage 1	2	9	5	22	53	8	-1.26
	Stage 2	3	8	4	24	50	10	-1.23
Violence in private between partners is nobody's business but their own	Stage 1	8	14	7	19	50	1	-0.89
	Stage 2	5	15	7	25	46	1	-0.94
Sometimes men can have a good reason for hitting their partners	Stage 1	4	13	4	11	66	2	-1.26
	Stage 2	2	12	3	16	65	2	-1.31
Men who hit their partners can be prosecuted in court	Stage 1	74	18	3	1	2	3	+1.66
	Stage 2	60	32	1	1	2	4	+1.53
It is only those types of cases of domestic violence where one partner is badly beaten up that are against the law	Stage 1	7	9	4	18	55	6	-1.12
	Stage 2	8	13	2	23	47	7	-0.95
There should be more services provided for those suffering from domestic violence	Stage 1	67	21	4	2	3	4	+1.53
	Stage 2	62	27	3	2	1	4	+1.52

It is not entirely clear why these slight changes in public attitudes should have occurred. It is possible, however, that as the commercial became more familiar to viewers, some may have started to see it without taking in its key message. That said, public attitudes remain strongly in line with the main thrust of the campaign.

---

* Mean scores are based on a five point rating scale from 'agree strongly'=+2 to 'disagree strongly'=-2.

ANALYSIS OF CALLS MADE TO THE DOMESTIC VIOLENCE INFORMATION LINE

Network Scotland

INTRODUCTION

Network Scotland Ltd was commissioned by the Information Directorate for The Scottish Office Crime Prevention Unit to provide a literature ordering service to support the Domestic Violence advertising campaign.

The aim of the campaign was to highlight the fact that domestic violence is socially unacceptable and a criminal act.

The campaign was launched on Monday 20 June and ran until Friday 23 December 1994.

The premium number allocated to the Domestic Violence Information line was 0800 33 66 99. Lines were open 24 hours.

The objectives of the Domestic Violence Information line were to provide referral to those in need of urgent help and to send out an information pack to anyone concerned about domestic violence.

STATISTICAL BREAKDOWN

The information contained within this report is in tabular form, and includes the following:

TABLE 1   Pack Requests

TABLE 2   Sex of Caller

TABLE 3.1   Region   Strathclyde, Lothian, Central
TABLE 3.2   Region   Tayside, Highlands & Islands, Grampian
TABLE 3.3   Region   Fife, Borders, Dumfries & Galloway
TABLE 3.4   Other   England, Northern Ireland, Wales

TABLE 4   Percentage Comparison of Callers with Regional Population

TABLE 5   Source of Number

TABLE 1   Pack Requests

Week	Date	No of Calls	No of Pack Requests	Pack Requests as a % of Total Calls
1	20/ 6/94 - 26/ 6/94	1,618	320	20%
2	27/ 7/94 - 3/ 7/94	967	115	12%
3	4/ 7/94 - 10/ 7/94	790	110	14%
4	11/ 7/94 - 17/ 7/94	786	98	12%
5	18/ 7/94 - 24/ 7/94	636	60	9%
6	25/ 7/94 - 31/ 7/94	564	24	4%
7	1/ 8/94 - 7/ 8/94	493	42	9%
8	8/ 8/94 - 14/ 8/94	381	28	7%
9	15/ 8/94 - 21/ 8/94	369	24	7%
10	22/ 8/94 - 28/ 8/94	438	39	7%
11	29/ 8/94 - 4/ 9/94	377	25	7%
12	5/ 9/94 - 11/ 9/94	340	30	9%
13	12/ 9/94 - 18/ 9/94	303	0	0
14	19/ 9/94 - 25/ 9/94	293	6	2%
15	26/ 9/94 - 2/ 9/94	298	2	1%
16	3/10/94 - 9/10/94	420	30	7%
17	10/10/94 - 16/10/94	407	40	10%
18	17/10/94 - 23/10/94	448	15	3%
19	24/10/94 - 30/10/94	494	14	3%
20	31/10/94 - 6/11/94	375	11	3%
21	7/11/94 - 13/11/94	494	24	5%
22	14/11/94 - 20/11/94	462	17	4%
23	21/11/94 - 27/11/94	331	14	4%
24	28/11/94 - 4/12/94	292	12	4%
25	5/12/94 - 11/12/94	337	12	4%
26	12/12/94 - 18/12/94	318	16	5%
27	19/12/94 - 23/12/94	163	11	7%
TOTAL	20/ 6/94 - 23/12/94	13,194	1,139	9%

TABLE 2   Sex of Caller

Week	No of Packs	Male		Female	
		Actual	%	Actual	%
1	320	79	25%	241	75%
2	115	25	22%	90	78%
3	110	39	35%	71	65%
4	98	9	9%	89	91%
5	60	13	22%	47	78%
6	24	7	29%	17	71%
7	42	12	29%	30	71%
8	28	6	12%	22	79%
9	24	7	29%	17	71%
10	39	11	28%	28	72%
11	25	9	36%	16	64%
12	30	6	20%	24	80%
13	0	0	0	0	0
14	6	0	0	6	100%
15	2	1	50%	1	50%
16	30	7	23%	23	77%
17	40	12	30%	28	70%
18	15	3	20%	12	80%
19	14	4	29%	10	75%
20	11	2	18%	9	82%
21	24	8	33%	16	67%
22	17	5	29%	12	71%
23	14	2	14%	12	86%
24	12	8	67%	4	33%
25	12	1	8%	11	92%
26	16	6	37%	10	63%
27	11	3	27%	8	73%
TOTAL	1,139	285	25%	854	75%

REFERRALS MADE TO SCOTTISH WOMEN'S AID

The following table shows the number of referrals to 14 of the 38 Scottish Women's Aid groups for the years 1993/4 and 1994/5 (the figures for the remaining groups are not, as yet, available). These show an increase of 3,382 (47%) over the period during which the domestic violence media campaign was running - a much larger increase than over any previous 12 month period. If the other 22 groups show similar increases, the total referrals for 1994/95 will be around 9,000 higher than those for 1993/94. Although it is clearly not possible to establish a direct causal link on the baisis of this information, it seems likely that this increase is at least partly due to the campaign.

Referrals to selected local groups: Scottish Women's Aid, 1993/94 and 1994/95

Name of Group	Referrals 1993/94	Referrals 1994/95
Clackmannan	567	749
Dumfries	934	1203
Dunfermline	642	829
East Kilbride	359	452
East Lothian	475	514
Falkirk	1298	2087
Inverness	429	580
Midlothian	270	50
Ross-shire	149	350
Shakti	217	460
Stirling	612	1016
Strathkelvin	664	781
W.Lothian & Livingston	562	990
Western Isles	68	117
Total	7246	10628

CRU RESEARCH - RECENTLY PUBLISHED WORK

The Measurement of Changes in Road Safety : A Consultant's Report by the Ross Silcock Partnership. (1991) *(£5.00)*

Socio-legal Research in the Scottish Courts - Volume 2 : Michael Adler and Ann Millar. (1991) *(£4.00)*

Crime Prevention in Scotland - Findings from the 1988 British Crime Survey : David M Allen and Douglas Payne. (1991) *(£4.00)*

The Public and the Police in Scotland - Findings from the 1988 British Crime Survey : David M Allen and Douglas Payne. (1991) *(£4.00)*

Ethnic Minorities in Scotland : Patten Smith (Social and Community Planning Research). (1991) *(£8.50)*

Adoption and Fostering - The Outcome of Permanent Family Placements in Two Scottish Local Authorities. (1991) *(£5.50)*

Adoption Services in Scotland - A Summary : Recent Research Findings and their Implications: John Triseliotis (Edinburgh University). (1991) *(£4.00)*

Children with Epilepsy and their Families - Needs and Services : A Laybourn and M Hill (Glasgow University). (1991) *(£4.00)*

Community Ownership in Glasgow - An Evaluation : David Clapham, Keith Kintrea and Leslie Whitefield (Centre for Housing Research, Glasgow University), Frances Macmillan and Norman Raitt (Norman Rait Architects, Edinburgh). (1991) *(£12.50)*

Small Claims in the Sheriff Court in Scotland - An Assessment of the Use and Operation of Procedure : Helen Jones, Alison Platts, Jacqueline Tombs (CRU); Cowan Irvine, James McManus (University of Dundee); Kenneth Miller, Alan Paterson (University of Strathclyde). (1991) *(£5.00)*

Physical Evaluation of Community Ownership Schemes : Frances Macmillan and Norman Raitt (Norman Rait Architects, Edinburgh). (1991) *(£10.00)*

The Impact of Environmental Design Upon the Incidence and Type of Crime - A Literature Review : Jonathan Bannister (Centre for Housing Research, Glasgow University). (1991) *(£5.00)*

Preventing Vehicle Theft - A Policy-Oriented View of the Literature : Ronald V Clarke (State University of New Jersey). (1991) *(£4.00)*

The Location of Alcohol Use by Young People - A Review of the Literature : Neil Hutton (School of Law, Strathclyde University). (1991)

Setting up Community Care Projects - A Practice Guide: Anne Connor. (1991)

Local Authority Housing Stock Transfers : Tom Duncan

(The Planning Exchange, Glasgow). (1991) *(£4.50)*

Competitive Tendering in Scotland - A Survey of Satisfaction with Local Authority Services : A Consultant's Report by The MVA Consultancy. (1991) *(£4.00)*

Public Attitudes to the Environment in Scotland : Diana Wilkinson and Jennifer Waterton. (1991) *(£4.00)*

Text Creation in the Scottish Office - The Experience, Expectations and Perceptions of the Users and Providers of Services: (A report on surveys of four groups of Scottish Office staff carried out by The Special Projects Branch of The Scottish Office Central Research Unit as part of an Efficiency Scrutiny of Text Creation in The Scottish Office): Hugh Gentleman and Susan A Hughes. (1992)

Where the Time Goes - The Allocation of Administration and Casework Between Client Groups in Scottish Departments of Social Work : John Tibbit and Pauline Martin. (1992) *(£4.00)*

Financial Management of Mentally Incapacitated Adults - Characteristics of Curatories : Fiona Rutherdale. (1992) *(£4.00)*

Evaluation of the Care and Repair Initiative in Scotland - Study Report : PIEDA and Norman Rait Architects. (1992) *(£5.00)*

Register of Research (1992-93 Edition) : (1992)

The Hidden Safety Net ? - Mental Health Guardianship: Achievements and Limitations : Carole Moore, Anne Connor, Pauline Martin and John Tibbitt. (1992) *(£5.00)*

Crime in Scotland - Findings from the 1988 British Crime Survey : Douglas Payne. (1992) *(£4.00)*

Crime and the Quality of Life - Public Perceptions and Experiences of Crime in Scotland: Findings from the 1988 British Crime Survey : Richard Kinsey and Simon Anderson. (1992) *(£4.00)*

The Deferred Sentence in Scotland : Linda Nicolson. (1992) *(£5.00)*

Social Work Department Reviews of Children in Care : Andrew Kendrick and Elizabeth Mapstone. (1992) *(£10.00)*

Retail Impact Assessment Methodologies : Consultant's Report by Drivers Jonas, Glasgow. (1992) *(£6.00)*

Section 50 Agreements : Consultant's Report by Jeremy Rowan Robinson and Roger Durman. (1992) *(£6.00)*

Evaluation of Scottish Road Safety Year 1990: Jennifer Waterton. (1992) *(£5.00)*

The Witness in the Scottish Criminal Justice System : Anne Stafford and Stewart Asquith. (1992) *(£4.00)*

Good Practice in Housing Management - A Literature Review : Mary Taylor & Fiona Russell, Dept. of Applied Social Science, Dr Rob Ball , Dept. of Management Science, University of Stirling (in association with The Institute of Housing in Scotland). (1992) *(£4.00)*

Sexual History and Sexual Character Evidence in Scottish Sexual Offence Trials - A Study of Scottish Court Practice under ss. 141A/141B and 346A/346B of the Criminal Procedure (Scotland) Act 1975 as inserted by the Law Reform (Miscellaneous Provisions)(Scotland) Act 1985 s. 36 : Beverley Brown, Michelle Burman and Lynn Jamieson. (1992) *(£4.50)*

Neighbourhood Watch - A Literature Review : Louise Brown. (1992) *(£4.00)*

Strathclyde Police Red Light Initiative - Accident Monitor : MVA Consultancy in association with Jennifer Waterton. (1992) *(£5.00)*

The Rent to Mortgage Scheme in Scotland : Helen Kay and Jeremy Hardin. (1992) *(£4.00)*

Probation In Scotland - Policy and Practice : Roslyn Ford, Jason Ditton and Ann Laybourn. (1992) *(£5.00)*

The Probation Alternative - Case Studies in the Establishment of Alternative to Custody Schemes in Scotland: Anne Creamer, Linda Hartley and Bryan Williams. (1992) *(£5.00)*

The Probation Alternative - A Study Of The Impact of Four Enhanced Probation Schemes On Sentencing: Anne Creamer, Linda Hartley and Bryan Williams. (1992) *(£5.00)*

Evaluation of Compulsory Competitive Tendering for Local Authority Services : Richard Evans. (1992) *(£4.00)*

The Review of Residential Child Care in Scotland - The Three Supporting Research Studies : Andrew Kendrick, Sandy Fraser, Moira Borland and Juliet Harvey. (1992) *(£5.00)*

Education in and out of School - The Issues and the Practice in Inner Cities and Outer Estates : John MacBeath. (1992) *(£5.50)*

The Use of Judicial Separation : Alison Platts. (1992) *(£4.00)*

Policing in the City - Public, Police and Social Work : Richard Kinsey. (1993) *(£4.50)*

Counting Travellers in Scotland - The 1992 Picture : Hugh Gentleman. (1993) *(£4.50)*

Crime Prevention and Housebreaking in Scotland: David McAllister, Susan Leitch and Douglas Payne. (1993) *(£4.00)*

Supporting Victims of Serious Crime: Rebbecca Dobash, Pat McLauglin and Russell Dobash. (1993) *(£4.00)*

Prohibiting the Consumption of Alcohol in Designated Areas: Janet Ruiz. (1993) *(£4.50)*

Appeals in the Scottish Criminal Courts: Ann Millar. (1993) *(£4.50)*

The Attitudes of Young Women Drivers to Road Safety: Cragg, Ross & Dawson Ltd. (1993) *(£5.00)*

The Management of Child Abuse - A Longitudinal Study of Child Abuse in Glasgow: Ann Laybourn and Juliet Harvey. (1993) *(£5.00)*

Supporting Victims in the Criminal Justice System - A study of a Scottish sheriff Court: Rosemary I Wilson. (1993) *(£4.00)*

Consideration of the Mental State of Accused Persons at the Pre-Trial and Pre-Sentencing Stages: G. D.L. Cameron, J. J. McManus. (1993) *(£4.00)*

Process & Preference - Assessment of Older People for Institutional Care: Elaine Samuel, Sue Brace, Graham Buckley and Susan Hunter. (1993) *(£5.50)*

Untying the Knot: Characteristics of Divorce in Scotland: Sue Morris, Sheila Gibson and Alison Platts. (1993) *(£5.00)*

The Practice of Arbitration in Scotland 1986-1990: Dr Fraser P Davidson. (1993) *(£5.00)*

Police Specialist Units for the Investigation of Crimes of Violence Against Women and Children In Scotland: Ms M Burman and Ms S Lloyd. (1993) *(£5.00)*

Local Authority Housing Waiting Lists in Scotland: Sarah Dyer. (1993) *(£4.50)*

The Right to Buy in Scotland - An Assessment of the Impact of the First Decade of the Right to Buy: Karen MacNee. (1993) *(£4.00)*

A Better Start - Social Work Service Projects for Homeless Young People (1993): Anne Conner and Debbie Headrick.
Part 1: The Experience of The Scottish Office Rooflessness Report
Part 2: The Scottish Office Rooflessness Initiative - Background and Research Findings

The Effects of Privatisation of the Scottish Bus Group and Bus Deregulation: Consultant's Report by The Transport Operations Research Group, Newcastle University. (1993) *(£3.00)*

The Voluntary Sector and the Environment: Alistair McCulloch, Seaton Baxter and John Moxen. (1993) *(£3.00)*

Social Work Responses to the Misuse of Alcohol - A Literature Review: Murray Simpson, Bryan Williams and Andrew Kendrick. (1993) *(£4.50)*

Socio - legal Research in the Scottish Courts Vol 3 : (eds)Michael Adler, Ann Millar & Sue Morris (1993)*(£5.00)*

Process and Preference - Assessment of Older People for Institutional Care: Elaine Samuel, Sue Brace, Graham Buckley and Susan Hunter. (1993) *(£5.50)*

Review of Retailing Trends: John Dawson. (1994) *(£7.50)*

Empty Public Sector Dwellings in Scotland - A Study of Empty Public Sector Housing in Scotland in 1992: Alan Murie, Sally Wainwright and Keith Anderson, School of Planning and Housing, Edinburgh College of Art/ Heriot-Watt University. (1994) *(£5.50)*

An Evaluation of "Cars Kill" Television Commercial: Research carried out on behalf of the Scottish Road Safety Campaign by System Three Scotland. (1994) *(£5.00)*

The Code of Guidance on Homelessness in Scotland - Local Authority Policies and Practice: Richard Evans, Nicholas Smith, Caroline Bryson and Nicola Austin. (1994) *(£6.50)*

Operating Bail - Decision Making Under the Bail etc. (Scotland) Act 1980: Fiona Paterson and Claire Whittaker. (1994) *(£15.95 from HMSO)*

Literature Review of Rural Issues: Karen MacNee. (1994) *(£5.00)*

Review of Scottish Coastal Issues: Consultant's Report by Peter R Burbridge and Veronica Burbridge. (1994) *(£5.00)*

Detention and Voluntary Attendance of Suspects at Police Stations: The MVA Consultancy. (1994) *(£5.00)*

Police User Surveys in Scotland: Dr Nicholas R Fyfe. (1994) *(£5.00)*

Evaluation of The Scottish Road Safety Campaign's Initiatives in Relation to the Year of the Eldery : Resarch carried out on behalf of the Scottish Road Safety Campaign by the MVA Consultancy. (1994) *(£5.00)*

Criminal Justice and Related Services for Young Adult Offenders : Stewart Asquith and Elaine Samuel. (1994) *(£11.95 from HMSO)*

Neighbourhood Disputes in the Criminal Justice System R. E. MacKay and S.R. Moody with Fiona Walker. (1994) *(£5.00)*

Attitudes of Scottish Drivers Towards Speeding - 1994 Survey : A Survey of Scottish Drivers conducted by Market Research Scotland Ltd on behalf of the Scottish Office. (1994) *(£5.00)*

A Review Of the Use Classes Order : Janet Brand (Strathclyde University) in association with David Bryce and Niall McClure (James Barr & Son, Chartered Surveyors). (1994) *(£5.00)*

Review of Census Applications : Pauline Martin. (1994) *(£5.00)*

Monetary Penalties in Scotland : Linda Nicholson. (1994) *(£13.95 from HMSO)*

Multi-Party Actions In Scotland : Dr. Christine Barker, Professor Ian D Willock and Dr. James J McManus. (1994) *(£5.00)*

Diversion from Prosecution to Psychiatric Care: Dr Peter Duff and Michelle Burman. (1994) *(£5.00)*

Opening and Reopening Adoption - Views From Adoptive Families: Linda Paterson (Abridged by Malcolm Hill). (1994) *(£5.00)*

The Use of The Judicial Examination Procedure in Scotland: Susan Leitch. (1994) *(£5.00)*

A Fine on Time - The Monitoring and Evaluation of the Pilot Supervised Attendance Order Schemes: Louise Brown. (1994) *(£4.00)*

Use of Controlled Drugs in Scotland - Findings from the 1993 Scottish Crime Survey: Richard Hammersley, Behavioural Sciences Group, University of Glasgow. (1994) *(£5.00)*

Evaluation of the Safer Edinburgh Project: James K Carnie. (1994) *(£5.00)*

Dundee NE Safer Cities Project 1994 Household Survey Report:H.R. Jones, D.E. Short and W.G. Berry, Department of Geography,The University,Dundee. (1994) *(£5.00)*

Child Sexual Abusers: Lorraine Waterhouse, Russell P Dobash and James Carnie. (1994) *(£6.00)*

Case Finding for Care Management for Elderly People - A Study of Existing Information Sources: Alex Robertson, Colin Currie and Eileen Brand. (1994) *(£5.00)*

The Role of The Mental Health Officer : Marion Ulas , Fiona Myers and Bill Whyte, Department of Social Policy and Social Work, Edinburgh University. (1994) *(£6.00)*

An Evaluation of Community Involvement in The Whitfield Partnership : Andrew McArthur, Annette Hastings and Alan McGregor, Training and Employment Research Unit, Glasgow University. (1994) *(£5.00)*

An Evaluation of Community Involvement in The Ferguslie Park Partnership : William Roe Associates. (1994) *(£5.00)*

Living in Castlemilk : Anne Corden and Mhairi Mackenzie with Claire Norris. (1994) *(£5.00)*

Perceptions of Drug Control Problems and Policies -A Comparison of Scotland and Holland in the 1980's : Sally Haw and Jason Ditton. (1995) *(£5.00)*

**What Works in Situational Crime Prevention ?
A Literature Review :** Linda Nicholson. (1995) *(£5.00)*

Deprived Areas in Scotland : George Duguid. (1995) *(£5.00)*

Live Television Link - An Evaluation of its Use by Child Witnesses in Scottish Criminal Trials : Kathleen Murray. (1995) *(£7.00)*

Sustainable Development - What it Means to the General Public : Ewen McCaig and Charlie Henderson (The MVA Consultancy). (1995) *(£5.00)*

Information Needs of Victims: The MVA Consultancy. *(1995) (£5.00)*

Implementation and Monitoring of the Children Act 1989 Part X and Section 19: Maureen Buist. (1995) *(£5.00)*

Social Work Placements in Scottish Local Authorities: Fiona M Fraser. (1995) *(£5.00)*

Running The Red - An Evaluation of The Strathclyde Police Red Light Camera Initiative: The MVA Consultancy. (1995) *(£5.00)*

Feuing Conditions in Scotland: Professor D. J. Cusine and M's J. Egan. (1995) *(£5.00)*

Review of Neighbour Notification: School of Planning & Housing, Edinburgh College of Art/ Heriot Watt University and Peter PC Allan Ltd. (1995) *(£5.00)*

Specialism in Private Legal Practice: Dr Karen Kerner. (1995) *(£5.00)*

Housing Management CCT in Rural Authorities: Douglas Johnston and Andrew Thomson, CSL-Touche Ross Management Consultants. (1995) *(£5.00)*

Management Options for Regional Parks - A Discussion Paper: Peter Scott Planning Services in association with Rosalind Pearson. (1995) *(£5.00)*

Accessing Enviromental Information in Scotland: John Moxen and Alistair McCulloch with Dorothy Williams and Seaton Baxter. (1995) *(£5.00)*

Enviromental Education - Is The Message Getting Through ? : Michele Corrado and Andrea Nove (MORI). (1995) *(£5.00)*

Residential Care in the Intergration of Child Care Services: Andrew Kendrick Dept. Of Social Work, University of Dundee. (1995) *(£5.00)*

Baseline Study of Public Knowledge and Perceptions of Local Goverment in Scotland: The MVA Consultancy. (1995) *(£5.00)*

An Evaluation of Scotland's National Tourist Routes: Colin Buchanan & Partners. (1995) *(£5.00)*

Public Interest and Private Grief - A Study of Fatal Accident Inquiries in Scotland: Simon Anderson, Susan Leitch and Sue Warner. (1995) *(£5.00)*

Pilgrim's Process ? - Defended Actions In The Sheriff's Ordinary Court: Sue Morris and Debbie Headrick. (1995) *(£5.00)*